Engd. by J. C. Buttre.

WILLIAM FOX.

FOUNDER OF THE FIRST SUNDAY SCHOOL SOCIETY.
Sept. 7th 1785.

Eng[d] by J. C. Buttre.

ROBERT RAIKES,

FOUNDER OF SUNDAY SCHOOLS.

1781-2.

THE RISE AND PROGRESS OF SUNDAY SCHOOLS

A Biography

OF

ROBERT RAIKES

AND

WILLIAM FOX.

BY

JOHN CARROLL POWER.

New-York:

SHELDON & COMPANY, 335 BROADWAY.

BOSTON: GOULD & LINCOLN.

MDCCCLXIII.

J. H. Tobitt, *Printer and Stereotyper*,
1 Franklin Square.

C. S. Westcott, *Printer*,
79 John Street.

TO THE

SUPERINTENDENTS,

TEACHERS, SCHOLARS,

AND OTHER

FRIENDS OF SABBATH SCHOOLS,

WHEREVER FOUND,

THIS VOLUME

IS

Most Respectfully Dedicated,

BY

THE AUTHOR.

OUR AUTHORITY.

"Gather the people together, men, and women, and children, and the stranger that is within thy gates, that they may hear, and that they may learn, and fear the Lord your God; and observe to do all the words of this law; And that their children, which have not known anything, may hear, and learn to fear the Lord your God."—Deut. xxxi. 12, 13.

"Train up a child in the way he should go, and when he is old he will not depart from it."—Prov. xxii. 6.

"Suffer little children to come unto Me, and forbid them not, for of such is the kingdom of heaven."—Matt. xix. 14. Mark x. 14. Luke xviii. 16.

PREFACE.

About thirty years ago, while attending the first Sabbath School of which I have any recollection, in the village of Mt. Carmel, Kentucky, I took from its library a small volume entitled "A Memoir of William Fox, Founder of the Sunday School Society." I read it, returned it to the library, and treasuring up some of its truths have never forgotten them. Since that time I have often mentioned some of the facts narrated in it, but seldom found, even among ministers of the gospel, any who seemed to have the least knowledge of the man, the book, or the historic information it contained. I never saw another copy of it until the summer of 1858. Having occasion to spend about three months in the city of Philadelphia, through the kindness of a friend I gained access to the old Philadelphia Library, founded by Benjamin Franklin, and spent many hours poring over its ancient volumes. Running my eye over the catalogue one day, I saw the title of the little book I had read so long before. I called for it, and upon exam-amination found it to be a copy of the same edition I had seen in my boyhood, and that it was published in the city of London, A. D. 1831. I then went to the rooms of the American Sunday School Union, not doubting that they had republished it, but was unable to find it. I continued my search by going to all the principal depositories of Sunday School books, to the number of about twenty, without finding the book, or a man that was acquainted with it. I then inquired for a biography of Robert Raikes—went nearly the same round, and at last entered a house that could get a copy for me by sending to the Methodist Book Concern, at New York—that establishment having republished Lloyd's Life of Raikes from a London edition. I found it so meagre and unsatisfactory as a history of the origin of Sunday Schools, that I returned to the Library hoping to purchase the memoir of William Fox. It being contrary to their rules to sell any book unless they had a duplicate, I could not get it in that way; but was permitted by the librarian to take it to my rooms, where I copied it entire.

I continued my inquiries into a history of the origin of Sunday Schools without any other object in view than to satisfy myself. The more I studied it, the more disjointed and fragmentary I found the whole subject.

After returning home it occurred to me that a History of Sunday Schools was needed, and would no doubt be acceptable to the Christian public if properly prepared. The materials I knew to be abundant, but to collect them would require time and labor. The next thought that presented itself was the importance of corresponding with the descendants of Messrs. Raikes and Fox. My first letter of inquiry was addressed to Dr. R. Shelton McKenzie, at that time literary editor of "The Press," in Philadelphia—a gentleman as much distinguished for his urbanity and kindness as for his critical acumen and thorough knowledge of the literary world. I received from him satisfactory answers to all my questions, with additional information and kind offers of assistance and encouragement to go forward. From him I also received the address of some of the Raikes family.

After accumulating materials from books, papers and correspondents, the plan which seemed to me most natural was to give, in the first chapter, an outline of the efforts to establish Sunday Schools prior to Mr. Raikes' time; in the second, sketch the life of Mr. Raikes previous to his publishing the first notice of his Schools; in the third, draw the life of Mr. Fox previous to the time he first met with the notice Mr. Raikes gave of his Schools, and commenced a correspondence with him; and then to use that correspondence with other materials, for the double purpose of continuing their Biography and making it a History of Sunday Schools, and after the death of both to devote one more chapter to each of them, and then close by bringing the History down to the end of their lives. The extensive correspondence I have used may be somewhat tedious, but I felt that the most accurate account of Sunday Schools could be given in the language of those who were the most prominent actors in making that History.

And now, while a portion of the people of Great Britain and our own land are indulging in jealousies and bickerings on account of the suffering occasioned by the great conflict in which our nation is engaged, it affords true pleasure to one American to place in order a History of the labors of two of the most noble sons of England in organizing an institution that has already conferred incalculable benefits upon both countries, and is destined to bless the Church and through it the world down to the end of time.

Fully aware that this, like all other human productions, is imperfect, but believing it will fill a vacancy in Christian literature, and hoping it may meet the MASTER'S approval, it is now offered to the public.

J. C. P.

DAVENPORT, Iowa, 1863.

A REQUEST.

The writer will feel under very great obligations to all persons who may notice this offering to Sabbath School literature, either in a public or private way, if they will send him a copy of such notice. The more acute the criticisms, the more desirable it is to secure a copy of them. Having been about five years collecting and arranging the facts now presented, it is his desire to collate and revise them until it shall be, if not already, a standard history of the origin of Sabbath Schools, and their organization into Societies.

Address

J. C POWER,
Davenport,
Iowa.

CONTENTS.

PAGE

CHAPTER VIII.

CHAPTER IX.

CHAPTER X.

CHAPTER XI.

CHAPTER XV.

CHAPTER XVI.

CHAPTER XVII.

BIOGRAPHY

OF

RAIKES AND FOX.

CHAPTER I.

THE germ of Sabbath Schools may be found in the Mosaic dispensation. The Sabbath was instituted as a day of rest, and for the worship of the true God, which could be acceptably rendered by those only who were instructed with regard to their duty to him and to each other.

When the rite of the Passover was instituted, directions were given to instruct the children when they asked the meaning of the service, that "It is the sacrifice of the Lord's Passover, who passed over the houses of the children of Israel in Egypt, when he smote the Egyptians and delivered our houses." Ex. xii. 27.

Moses exhorted the people not to forget what they had seen of God's dealings with them, but teach them their sons, and their sons' sons. And when he knew that the time of his departure was at hand, he delivered to Joshua his successor, this charge—" Gather the people together, men, and women, and children, and the stranger that is within thy gates, that they may hear, and that they may learn, and fear the Lord your God, and observe to do all the words of this law; and that their children, which have not known anything, may hear, and learn to fear the Lord your God." Deut. xxxi. 12—13.

The prophet Isaiah, after describing in glowing language the sufferings to be endured, and the triumphs to be achieved by the Messiah upon his advent into the world, and the conquest to be gained by Mount Zion, the Church of God, thus speaks of her coming glory—" And all thy children shall be taught of the Lord, and great shall be the peace of thy children." Isa. liv. 13.

The divinely-inspired Zechariah, speaking of the restoration of Jerusalem, which is yet to take place under the influence of the teachings of Christianity, says it shall be called " a city of truth." The outline of the picture thus presented to the mind, he fills up by saying, " And the streets of the city shall be full of boys and girls playing in the streets thereof." Zech. viii. 5.

It is well known that every Jewish synagogue was called a school, and all the children attended them on the Sabbath, to receive such instruction as children could understand—thus early were Sabbath Schools in fact, though not in name, established.

A modern writer says that "When Jesus was only twelve years old, on one of his annual visits to the temple with his parents, he ceased to be a scholar, and took his rightful place as a teacher. Previous to this he enjoyed no more religious advantages than other children of devout parents in that nation. Indeed the principle of Sabbath Schools, the religious education of children, has been perhaps the strongest power to produce that perpetual miracle, the preservation of the Jews as a distinct people among all the nations of the earth. By Sabbath Schools God prepared the way for the Messiah. Without Sabbath Schools, the world could not have received the Christ."

"I need not review the early history of the Christian Church to show you that the Apostles, the .earliest preachers, and the earliest Christian societies, enjoined and encouraged the principle of what we call Sabbath Schools. All know that a large portion of every primitive Christian society was composed of catechumens, consisting of the children of Christian parents, and persons of all ages who wished to learn the principles of Christianity. They met on the Lord's day, and were instructed by the elders, and doubtless by others, in the elements of the Christian religion. The idea of the Sabbath School is not new—were it less than a hundred years old, I should doubt its usefulness as a permanent institution. It cannot be possible that any proper and needed department of activity in the Church of Christ has been wholly neglected for nearly two thousand years. Sabbath Schools were in fact a revival, an enlargement, and an improvement of what has always formed an essential part of the machinery of the Church of Christ."

Coming down nearer to our own times, we learn that when the giant mind of Martin Luther broke the fetters of superstitious tradition that bound the Christian world in that age, and took the Bible alone as the rule of his faith and practice, there was nothing more natural than that he should wish the same blessings extended to others—and thus we find in the language of Dr. Sears, that in the year 1527 he "laid the foundation of the magnificent organization of schools to which Germany owes so much of her present fame."

This provision for mental culture did not satisfy him, for he at the same time established religious schools on the Lord's-day, "devoted to the study of a Biblical catechism, singing the praises of God, and the great duty of prayer." In other words, he instituted Sabbath Schools. Previous to the year 1584, Charles Borromeo, Archbishop of Milan, organized Sabbath Schools, first in the Cathedral of Milan, and after that throughout his diocese, which extended over a considerable portion of Lombardy.

In 1688 the Rev. Joseph Alleine, author of the "Alarm to the Unconverted," had a Sabbath School in connexion with his church at Taunton, Somerset shire, England. In 1767 the Rev. John Frederick Oberlin became pastor of Waldbach in the Ban de la Roche, France. He then established the first infant schools known. He also required the children from the five villages composing his parish, to attend the parish church every Sabbath in rotation, "to sing the hymns they had learned, to recite the religious lessons they had committed to memory during the week, and to receive instruction from the pastor." Mr. Oberlin was so conscientious in his anti-slavery principles, that he would voluntarily deprive himself of the use of sugar, coffee, or any other article he knew to be the product of slave labor.

Dr. Stevens, in his History of Methodism, says—"As early as 1769, a young Methodist, Miss Hannah Ball, [another author mentions her as an Episcopalian—both may be correct, for all Methodists were then Episcopalians] established a Sunday School in High Wycombe, [England,] and was instrumental in training many children in the knowledge of the Holy Scriptures."

In 1773, a clergyman by the name of Kindermaun formed a Sabbath School in a Bohemian village in which he settled. Others followed his example, and it produced such good results that Maria Theresa, Empress of Austria, conferred upon him a title of nobility as a reward for his services.

Many places in America claim the honor of having Sabbath schools prior to 1781. In fact as early as 1680, (a century before their general introduction,) the records of the Pilgrim's Church, at Plymouth, Massachusetts, then under the care of the Rev. John Robinson, show that a Sabbath School was organized at that time in connexion with the church.

A vote of the church in the form of a request is as follows—"That the Deacons of the Church be requested to assist the minister in teaching the children during the intermission on the Sabbath."

The claim comes from the city of Savannah, Georgia, that in 1737 the Rev. John Wesley instituted Sabbath Schools there, and that they were continued by the Rev. Charles Wesley and the Rev. George Whitefield.

Bethlehem, Connecticut, claims that in 1740 the Rev. Dr. Joseph Bellamy established a Sunday School in that town, which by adapting itself to the modern improvements in Sabbath Schools, has continued to the present time.

About the same year, (1740) the German Seventh-day Baptists at Ephrata, Lancaster County, Pennsylvania, commenced Sabbath Schools under the direction of Ludwig Strecker—these schools were in operation at the time of our Revolution.

A very able article on Sabbath Schools, by the Rev. John Douglas, D. D., appeared in the United Presbyterian Quarterly Review, Pittsburgh, Pa., in the July and October numbers for 1861. He quotes from the Free Church Magazine (Scotland) for 1844—

" Sabbath School teaching is of no recent origin in Scotland. That system of Sabbath School teaching, through the instrumentality of 'readers,' was devised by John Knox at the very beginning of the Reformation, and has always been, to some extent, practised in Scotland ever since. John Brown, the godly carrier, had in his day a Sabbath School at Priesthill. Even as a modern system it was not borrowed from England, as some imagine ; for schools were in existence at Glasgow and other places about the middle of the last century [1759.] They did not become common, however, till the beginning of this century."

After producing quite a formidable array of testimony, Mr. Douglas says—

" In these quotations there is evidence sufficient to satisfy every reasonable mind that schools for religious instruction on the Sabbath day have existed in Scotland since the year 1560. But we find additional corroboration in the laws of the Church of Scotland. In the year 1647 the Commisioners of Universities represented to the General Assembly that the overtures of 1643 for the visitation of schools and the advancement of learning were very much neglected ; whereupon the Assembly recommended to all Universities to be careful to take account of their scholars on the *Sabbath-day*, of the sermons, and of their lessons in the Catechism."

Mr. Douglas further says—

"We have the authority of the Rev. John Brown, D. D., of Langton, Berwickshire, Scotland, for saying that Sabbath Schools were known to exist in Glasgow and other places about the year 1707."

Dr. Brown, above alluded to, writing in 1837, says that the Rev. Dr. Burns, of the Barony Parish, Glasgow, had written to him several years before, that he was a scholar in the Sabbath school of that place in 1782. Dr. Brown says he had information from another source that a Sabbath School was in existence at Banorchy, Devinick, in Aberdeenshire, as far back as 1782. In both cases they were without the knowledge of any similar schools. Mr. Douglas gives many more facts of a similar character.

But the *Era* of Sabbath Schools dates from the year 1781 or 1782, when Robert Raikes commenced them in the city of Gloucester, England.

Allow me in this place to ask why it is that Luther, Borromeo, Alleine, Oberlin, Kindermaun, and others in Europe, and Robinson, the Wesleys, Bellamy, Strecker, and others in America, are passed by, and the entire honor conferred upon Robert Raikes as the founder of Sabbath Schools ? It may be answered that they failed and he was successful, and that success is always honored. But why did they fail, and why was he successful?

In answer to these questions it may be said, that in those early days the art of printing was in its infancy, so that books and other printed matter would have been difficult to obtain—but in the time of Mr. Raikes the art had so far advanced that books were comparatively cheap, giving a better opportunity to test the value of the schools. Christians too, were becoming more generally imbued with the true missionary spirit. Notwithstanding all these advantages, Sabbath Schools might and doubtless would have been again lost, (for they did cease to exist in Gloucester about the time of the death of Mr. Raikes,) had not other means been used to perpetuate them.

The grand cause of all these failures was the absence of any efforts to systematize the work with a view to its perpetuation and extension—consequently when the first mover in any given enterprise died, the work died, however self-sacrificing and persevering he might have been while living.

Mr. Raikes had gone further than any one who had preceded him in furnishing books, but there is no intimation whatever that he expected to leave any organized system of supply after his death, without which he certainly would never have been known as the Founder of Sunday Schools.

How then was this deficiency supplied? At the same time that Mr. Raikes was patiently attending his schools in Gloucester unknown to the rest of the world, there was a wholesale merchant in the city of London named William Fox, whose business required him to travel extensively over the kingdom, giving him an opportunity of witnessing the deplorable ignorance of the poorer classes of the people. Mr. Fox, moved with compassion at the sight of their degraded condition, attempted to devise some means of establishing a Society for supporting week-day schools throughout England, in which *poor children might be taught to read the Bible.* He went so far as to bring the subject before a business meeting of the church of which he was a Deacon, and had a committee appointed to investigate the subject, and to report at a future meeting. Before the time came for them to report, the first printed notice of Mr. Raikes' schools fell into his hands, and he immediately opened a correspondence with Mr. Raikes—and when the time came for the committee to report, Mr. Fox as chairman recommended that they proceed with the organization of their society, and that instead of the original name proposed, it be called "The Society for Promoting Sunday Schools throughout the British Dominions." The report was adopted, and after a few adjourned meetings, the society was organized Sept. 7, 1785.

It cannot detract from the value of the labors of

either Mr. Raikes or Mr. Fox to say that neither of them, unaided by the other, was likely to bring Sabbath Schools into general use.

And the happy combination of circumstances that brought them to a knowledge of each other's efforts, can be viewed in no other light than that of a plan of Divine Providence to give to the world, next to the Church, the most efficient of missionary organizations.

CHAPTER II.

For more than three centuries the name of Raikes has been associated with honorable positions in society and noble deeds in English history, as may be seen by the following genealogy taken from the writings of Burke, one of the English historians.—He appears to have quoted from another.

"The family of Raikes," says Bigland, "was settled at Kingston-upon-Hull, and other places in the county of York at a very remote period, as appears, not only by wills of the family proved in the prerogative court of York as early as the year 1507, but also by the ancient entries in the parochial register of Hull, which are so numerous, particularly in the reign of Elizabeth, that the necessary identification to justify insertion in the pedigrees of other ascending lines, cannot be strictly ascertained."

Of three brothers, Richard, Thomas and Robert, living in Hull in 1610, Thomas bore a prominent part in the important transactions of which that town was the scene at the commencement of the civil war.

Having first served in the office of Mayor in 1633, he was again elected in 1642, and during the siege, as appears by a minute dated September 3, 1643, at the election of mayor for the year to come, the burgesses assembled taking into consideration the mayor's (Thomas Raikes, Esq.) vigilance and carefulness of the town's affairs the year past, and his fidelity to the public cause, and the great danger that the town is now in, being at present strongly beleaguered by the Earl of Newcastle's forces, being nigh and daily shooting into the town with their great ordnance, earnestly prayed the mayor either to continue mayor as he is; or that he would be elected mayor again for the year to come.

He consented when [after] Lord Fairfax, Governor came [had come] into the assembly and requested him to do so, &c. The said Thomas Raikes died in 1662, and was buried in the Holy Trinity Church at Hull. He, as well as his brother Robert left issue, but their descendants in the male line appear to have become extinct before 1700. Their eldest brother, Richard Raikes, a merchant in Hull, had by his wife, Anne, living in 1640, twin sons, Richard and Joshua, and five daughters: Anne married in 1619 to Christopher Shore, Esq.; Hester married William Wilberforce, Esq.; Elizabeth married in 1630 to William Mather; Isabel married in 1638 to James Nettleton, Esq., and Alice married to Anthony Stephenson.

The Rev. Robert Raikes, the elder son, was vicar of

Hessle, county York, in 1640, and dying in 1671 left by his wife Jane three sons and three daughters. His eldest son, the Rev. Timothy Raikes, took his degree at St. John's College, Cambridge, in 1670, and was first, vicar of Tickhill, afterwards vicar of Hessle aforesaid. He died at Hessle, in 1722.

By Sarah, his wife, daughter of ——— Partridge, Esq., of the county of Gloucester, he had three sons, Robert, Richard, and Timothy, and two daughters.

From Timothy descends the family of Richard of St. Petersburg. The eldest son, Robert Raikes, settled at Gloucester, and died in 1759. He married Mary, daughter of the Rev. Richard Drew, of Nailsworth, in that county, and by her had one daughter, Mary, married to Francis Newby, Esq., of Heathfield Park, Sussex county, and five sons; Robert, the well known philanthropist and founder of Sunday Schools, who lived and died at Gloucester, [being one of them.] He married in 1767, Ann, only daughter of Thomas Trigge, Esq., of Newenham, and had six daughters and two sons. Robert Napier Raikes, Rector of Drayton, County Norfolk, born in Nov. 3, 1783. William Henly Raikes, Colonel in the Guards, born in 1785.

Robert Raikes, the philanthopist above refered to is the subject of this memoir. He was born in the city of Gloucester, England, Sept. 14, 1736.

As will be seen by the above genealogy, Robert

Raikes was the eldest son of a gentleman of the same name. His mother's maiden name was Mary Drew.

But little is known of the childhood and youth of Robert Raikes. The articles that have been published concerning him have been written without a due regard to the importance of the subject. Consequently they are deprived of those domestic incidents, that bear the same relation to biography, that condiments do to our food; and foreshadow in childhood what may be expected of the man.

He spent some time in the University of Cambridge but never graduated in any department of it, as he preferred being brought up to business. His father was the printer and publisher of a newspaper called the Gloucester Journal.

Mr. Raikes' father died when he was about twenty-one years of age, and he succeeded him in the publication of the Journal, which seems to have been kept up, more with a design to further some religious and political objects, than for the small profit it afforded; the family being in possession of an ample fortune he could thus indulge his tastes and inclinations.

When men are successful in worldly pursuits, or inherit fortunes from their ancestors, they are naturally inclined to indulge in ease, gratify selfish lusts and passions, and shut out from their minds and hearts the claims of their fellow beings less fortunate than themselves.

The actions of Robert Raikes convince us that selfishness was not the ruling passion with him, but that higher and more ennobling sentiments directed his footsteps, and made him feel that what he had was not his own but was entrusted to his care as a steward of his Heavenly Father to whom he must give an account.

In this sinful world objects of benevolence are always at hand, for those who are not wilfully blind. The first of these that are known to have called the attention of Mr. Raikes was the condition of those who were justly suffering for their crimes in the county work-house within the city of Gloucester. The work-house being part of the county jail, the persons committed by the magistrates between sessions of court for petty offences, associated through necessity with felons of the worst description. This prison was often crowded with criminals, and no appropriation made for feeding them, and there were but little means for them to procure food by labor. The efforts of John Howard, Miss Dix, and others of the same spirit, had not then, as now, influenced governments to recognize the claims of humanity in the most abandoned criminals, by providing for their physical comfort, at the same time that the safety of law abiding citizens demanded they should be suitably punished. Therefore these criminals were dependent chiefly upon the charity of those who visited the prison, either for business, curiosity, or pleasure.

To relieve them, and to render their situation at least endurable, Mr. Raikes employed his pen, his personal influence, and his property, to procure for them the necessaries of life. While engaged in these laudable efforts to ameliorate the condition of those who had violated the laws of their country, he became satisfied that ignorance was the stepping-stone to the crimes which made them objects of his notice. He therefore determined, if possible, to procure them some moral and religious instruction. In this he succeeded by encouraging in various ways those prisoners who were able to read. These, by being directed to proper books, improved both themselves and fellow-prisoners, and afforded great encouragement to Mr. Raikes to persevere in his benevolent design. He next procured for them a supply of such work as could be done within the prison walls, with a view to keeping their minds occupied, and also to encourage the formation of habits of industry.

While Mr. Raikes was engaged in these benevolent and praiseworthy efforts to relieve the suffering outcasts from civilized life, he was led to many serious reflections.

His mind is said to have been particularly affected by the sad consequences arising from the neglect, or rather entire absence of opportunities for early instruction among the poor. He was thus induced to indulge in a second project for their benefit, namely, the establishment of Sunday Schools, which is said to have been presented to his mind, by going into the suburbs of his native city, one morning in the latter part of 1781 or the beginning of 1782, for the purpose of hiring a gardener. The gardener being from home, Mr. Raikes awaited his return. While thus leisurely passing the time, a group of very noisy boys who had assembled in the street, attracted his attention. He asked the gardener's wife the cause of their being so neglected and depraved.

Without directly answering his questions, she told him that if he were to visit the place on the Sabbath, he would sympathize with the people of the neighborhood, for the noise and confusion was so great as to deprive them of the quiet enjoyment of that day.

He then inquired of her if there were any teachers who could be induced to give instruction to the children on the Sabbath, and was directed to those whom she supposed would be willing to engage in the work.

Mr. Raikes has been heard to say, that at this important juncture the word " Try " was so powerfully impressed upon his mind as to cause him to go forward without delay.

He immediately went and made an agreement with each of four female teachers to take charge of a certain number of these children on the next Sabbath—and this was the beginning of his Sunday Schools.

He continued his efforts, and enlisted others in the cause, until the Sunday Schools were increased to a considerable number in the vicinity of Gloucester—so much that on the third day of November, 1783, he published the following article in his paper, modestly putting forward those whom he had enlisted in the service, as the movers in the good work.

"Some of the clergy in different parts of this County, bent upon attempting a reform among the children of the lower classes, are establishing Sunday Schools for rendering the Lord's Day subservient to the ends of instruction, which has hitherto been prostituted to bad purposes. Farmers and other inhabitants of the towns and villages, complain that they receive more injury in their property on the Sabbath than all the week besides; this in a great measure proceeds from the lawless state of the younger class, who are allowed to run wild on that day, free from every restraint. To remedy this evil, persons duly qualified are employed to instruct those that cannot read—and those that may have learned to read, are taught the Catechism and conducted to church.

"By thus keeping their minds engaged, the day passes profitably and not disagreeably. In those parishes where this plan has been adopted, we are assured that the behaviour of the children is greatly civilized.

"The barbarous ignorance in which they had before lived being in some degree dispelled, they begin to give proofs that those persons are mistaken who consider the lower orders of mankind as incapable of improvement, and therefore think an attempt to reclaim hem impracticable, or at least not worth the trouble."

This being the first public notice given of Sunday Schools, it was copied into the London papers, in consequence of which numerous applications for information on the subject were addressed to Mr. Raikes and others living in the city of Gloucester.

Among the number, Colonel Townley, a gentleman of Lancashire, near Liverpool, seeing this paragraph going the rounds of the papers, wrote to the Mayor of Gloucester for further information on the subject. The annexed letter was written as a reply by Mr. Raikes:

GLOUCESTER, Nov. 25, 1783.

SIR—My friend the Mayor has just communicated to me the letter which you have honored him with, inquiring into the nature of Sunday Schools.

The beginning of the scheme was entirely owing to accident. Some business leading me one morning into the suburbs of the city where the lowest of the people—who are principally employed in the pin manufactory—chiefly reside, I was struck with concern at seeing a group of children, wretchedly ragged, at play in the street. I asked an inhabitant whether those children belonged to that part of the town, and lamented their misery and idleness. "Ah sir," said the woman to whom I was speaking, "could you take a view of this part of the town on a Sunday, you would be shocked indeed, for then the street is filled with multitudes of these wretches—who, released on that day from employment, spend their time in noise and riot, playing at chuck, and cursing and swearing in a manner so horrid as to convey to any serious mind an idea of hell rather than any other place.

"We have a clergyman—the Rev. Thomas Stock—minister of our parish, who has put some of them to school; but upon the Sabbath, they are all given up to follow their inclinations without restraint—as their parents, totally abandoned themselves, have no idea of instilling into the minds of their children, principles to which they themselves are entire strangers."

This conversation suggested to me that it would be at least a harmless attempt, if it were productive of no good, should some little plan be formed to check this deplorable profanation of the Sabbath. I then inquired of the woman if there were any decent, well-disposed women in the neighborhood who kept schools for teaching to read. I was presently directed to four. To these I applied, and made an agreement with them to receive as many children as I should send upon the Sunday, whom they were to instruct in reading, and the Church Catechism. For this I engaged to pay them each a shilling for their day's employment. The women seemed pleased with the proposal. I then waited on the clergyman before mentioned, and imparted to him my plan. He was so much satisfied with the idea that he engaged to lend his assistance by going around to the schools on a Sunday afternoon to examine the progress that was made, and to enforce order and decorum among such a set of little heathens.

This, sir, was the commencement of the plan—it is now about three* years since we began, and I wish you were here to make inquiry into the effect.

A woman who lives in a lane where I had fixed a school, told me some time ago that the place was quite a heaven upon Sundays, compared with what it used to be.

The numbers who have learned to read and say their Catechisms are so great that I am astonished at it. Upon the Sunday afternoon the mistresses take their scholars to church—a place into which neither they nor their ancestors ever entered with a view to the glory of God.

* This does not harmonize with the statement that the schools were commenced in the latter part of 1781 or beginning of '82—but we give both as we find them. P.

But what is more extraordinary, within this month these little ragamuffins have in great numbers taken it into their heads to frequent the early morning prayers, which are held every morning in the cathedral at seven o'clock. I believe there were near fifty this morning. They assembled at the house of one of the mistresses, and walk before her to church in as much order as a company of soldiers. I am generally at church, and after service they all come round me to make their bow—and if any animosities have arisen, to make their complaint.

The great principle I inculcate is to be kind and good-natured to each other—not to provoke one another—to be dutiful to their parents—not to offend God by cursing and swearing—and such little plain precepts as all may comprehend.

As my profession is that of a printer, I have printed a little book which I give amongst them ; and some friends of mine, subscribers to the Society for promoting Christian knowledge, sometimes make me a present of a parcel of Bibles, Testaments, &c., which I distribute as rewards to the deserving.

The success that has attended this scheme has induced one or two of my friends to adopt the plan, and set up Sunday Schools in other parts of the city—and now a whole parish has taken up the subject, so that I flatter myself in time the good effects will appear so conspicuous as to become generally adopted.

The number of children at present thus engaged on the Sabbath is between two and three hundred, and they are increasing every week, as the benefit is universally seen. I have endeavored to engage the clergy of my acquaintance that reside in their parishes. One has entered into the scheme with great fervor—and it was in order to excite others to follow the example that I inserted in my paper the paragraph which I suppose you saw copied into the London papers.

I cannot express to you the pleasure I often receive in discovering genius and innate good dispositions among this little multitude. It is botanizing in human nature. I have often, too, the satisfaction of receiving thanks from parents for the reformation they perceive in their children.

Often have I given them kind admonitions, which I always do in the mildest and gentlest manner. The going among them, doing them little kindnesses, distributing trifling rewards, and ingratiating myself with them, I hear, have given me an ascendency greater than I ever could have imagined; for I am told by their mistresses that they are very much afraid of my displeasure.

If you ever pass through Gloucester, I shall be happy to pay my respects to you, and to show you the effects of this effort at civilization. If the glory of God be promoted in any, even the smallest degree, society must reap some benefit. If good seed be sown in the mind at an early period of human life, though it shows itself not again for many years, it may please God at some future period to cause it to spring up, and to bring forth a plenteous harvest.

With regard to the rules adopted, I only required that they come to school on Sunday as clean as possible. Many were at first deterred because they wanted decent clothing, but I could not undertake to supply this defect. I argue, therefore, if you can loiter about, without shoes, and in a ragged coat, you may as well come to school, and learn what may tend to your good in that garb.

I reject none on that footing. All that I require are clean hands, clean face, and the hair combed; if you have no clean shirt, come in that which you have on. The want of decent apparel, at first, kept great numbers at a distance, but they now begin to grow wiser, and all are pressing to learn. I have had the good luck to procure places for some that were deserving, which has been of great use. You will understand that these children are from six years old to twelve or fourteen. Boys and girls above this age who have been totally undisciplined, are generally too refractory for this government. A reformation in society seems to me only practicable by establishing notions of duty, and practical habits of order and decorum at an early age. But whither am I running?

I am ashamed to see how much I have trespassed on your patience, but I thought the most complete idea of Sunday Schools, was to be conveyed to you by telling what first suggested the thought. The same sentiments would have arisen in your mind had they happened to have been called forth, as they were suggested to me.

I have no doubt that you will find great improvement to be made on this plan. The minds of men have taken great hold on that prejudice, that we are to do nothing on the Sabbath-day which may be deemed labor, and therefore we are to be excused from all application of mind as well as body. The rooting out of this prejudice is the point I aim at as my favorite object. Our Saviour takes particular pains to manifest that whatever tended to promote the health and happiness of our fellow-creatures, were sacrifices peculiarly acceptable on that day.

I do not think I have written so long a letter for some years. But you will excuse me, my heart is warm in the cause. I think this is the kind of reformation most requisite in this kingdom. Let our patriots employ themselves in rescuing their countrymen from that despotism, which tyrannical passions, and vicious inclinations, exercise over them, and they will find that true liberty and national welfare are more essentially promoted than by any reform in Parliament.

As often as I have attempted to conclude, some new idea has arisen. This is strange, as I am writing to a person whom I never have, and perhaps never may see; but I have felt that we think alike; I shall therefore only add my ardent wishes, that your views of promoting the happiness of society may be attended with every possible success, conscious that your own internal enjoyment will thereby be considerably advanced.

I have the honor, &c.,

R. RAIKES.

At Colonel Townley's request, this letter was published in the Gentleman's Magazine—a London periodical—for 1784, vol. 54—page 410; thus a knowledge of Sunday Schools was diffused throughout the kingdom.

Mr. Raikes very soon had occasion to answer other enquiries; among them one from Bradford in Yorkshire. His reply to that agrees in substance with the one you have just read, but as it shows how others were induced to favor Sunday Schools, it will not be amiss to place it before the reader in this connection; it was dated—

GLOUCESTER, June 5, 1784.

Having found four persons who had been accustomed to instruct children in reading, I engaged to pay the sum they required for receiving and instructing such children as I should send to them every Sunday. The children were to come soon after ten in the morning, and stay till twelve; they were then to go home, and return at one; and after reading a lesson they were to be conducted to church. After church they were to be employed repeating the catechism till half past five, and then to be dismissed with an injunction to go home without making a noise, and by no means to play in the street. This was the general outline of the regulation.

With regard to the parents, I went round, to remonstrate with them on the melancholy consequences that must ensue from a neglect of their children's morals. They alleged that their poverty rendered them incapable of cleaning, or clothing their children fit to appear either at school or at church; but this objection was obviated by a remark, that *if* they were clad in a garb fit to appear in the streets, I should not think it improper for a school, calculated to admit the poorest and most neglected. All that I required were clean faces, clean hands, and the hair combed.

In other respects, they were to come as their circumstances would admit. Many children began to show talents for learning, and a desire to be taught Little rewards, (such as books, combs, shoes, or some article of apparel,) were distributed among the most diligent; this excited an emulation. One or two clergymen gave their assistance by going round to the schools on the Sunday afternoon, to hear the children their catechism; this was of great consequence.

Another clergyman hears them their catechism once a quarter publicly in the church, and rewards their good behavior with some little gratuity.

They are frequently admonished to refrain from swearing; and certain boys who are distinguished by their decent behavior, are appointed to superintend the conduct of the rest, and make report of those that swear, call names, or interrupt the comfort of the other boys in their neighborhood. When quarrels have arisen, the aggressor is compelled to ask pardon, and the offended is enjoined to forgive.—The happiness that must arise to all from a kind, good-natured behavior, is often inculcated.

This mode of treatment has produced a wonderful change in the manners of these little savages. I cannot give a more striking instance, than I received the other day, from Mr. Church, a considerable manufacturer of hemp and flax, who employs great numbers of these children. I asked him whether he perceived any alteration in the poor children he employed. "Sir," says he, "the change could not have been more extraordinary in my opinion, had they been transformed from the shape of wolves and tigers, to that of men. In temper, disposition and manners, they could hardly be said to differ from the brute creation. But since the establishment of the Sunday Schools, they have seemed anxious to show that they are not the ignorant, illiterate creatures they were before. When they have seen a superior come, and kindly instruct and admonish them, and sometimes reward their good behavior, they are anxious to gain his friendship and good opinion. They are also become more tractable and obedient, and less quarrelsome and revengeful. In short, I never conceived that a reformation, so singular, could have been effected amongst the set of untutored beings I employ.

"From this little sketch of the reformation which has taken place, there is reason to hope, that a general establishment of Sunday Schools would, in time, make some change in the morals of the lower class. At least it might, in some measure, prevent them from growing worse, which at present, seems but too apparent." I am, Sir, &c,

R. RAIKES.

P. S.—The parish of St. Nicholas has lately established two schools ; and some gentlemen of this city have also set up others. To some of the school mistresses I give two shillings a week extra to take the children when they come from work during the week days.

It is so well known as scarcely to require being

mentioned by me, that Robert Raikes was born and brought up in the Protestant Episcopal Church, that he was strictly moral and upright in his character, and a punctual attendant upon all the services of the Church. But of his experimental application of its doctrines to himself we know but little , the information we have, however, leads us to the opinion that he did not fully appreciate the spirituality of its teachings ; in support of these views, we quote the following from an excellent little volume entitled, "Robert Raikes, his Sunday Schools, and his Friends," published in 1859 by the "American Baptist Publication Society."

The author of the above named work, hides his name behind the initials, J. B., but a friend who evidently knows whereof he affirms, says it was the Rev. Joseph Belcher, D. D. He was a native of England, and died in Philadelphia in the year 1860 at an advanced age ; but to the quotation :

"Of the strictly *religious* history of this eminent man, we know even less than we do of his early life. Forty years ago, we were well acquainted with a distinguished Christian gentleman in London, who was intimately acquainted with Mr. Raikes at the time he commenced Sabbath Schools ; and he was entirely convinced that his friend at that period was inexperienced in the religion of the heart; and that he was resting his expectations of eternal life on the moral ity of his conduct, and his observance of the forms of devotion."

The same writer continues :—" And with this accorded the testimony borne in the momoir of the Rev. Thomas English, an excellent Congregational minister, who died in 1809. This was to the effect that Mr Raikes's first thorough conviction of sin, and his first approach to the Cross of Christ for mercy, was the result of reading the fifty-third chapter of Isaiah to a little girl, one of his own Sunday Scholars."

Having a personal knowledge of unconverted teach ers being greatly blessed in giving instruction to a Sabbath School class, and believing that every aid should be extended to others under similar circumstances, I advise you, reader, before you go further, turn to that chapter, in the reading of which Mr Raikes was so greatly blessed. If you are a Christian it will add to your growth in grace, if unconverted it may lead you to embrace the Saviour you have long neglected.

This accurate description of the sufferings of the Saviour, written seven hundred years before it occured, is so striking that when read and compared with the same account in the gospels the cause for astonishment, is not, that Mr. Raikes was converted by it, but that thousands remain unconverted after having read it.

Having now brought the life of Mr. Raikes, as the

founder of Sunday Schools down to the point where the public attention is drawn to them by his letters, particularly the one to Colonel Townley, I shall say no more concerning him at present, but will devote the next chapter to the life of Mr. Fox.

CHAPTER III.

"The year 1732 will ever be memorable in the history of America, as giving birth to two of the most noble thunderbolts of her wars—George Washington and Francis Marion."

So wrote Peter Horry in his Life of Marion—and I think it would not be inappropriate to express the same idea here, but with a different application.

The year 1736 will ever be memorable in the history of Christianity, because it gave birth to two of the most noble philanthropists with whom the world has been blessed in any age—Robert Raikes and William Fox. They were born not only in the same year, but on the same day of the month, though not the same month, and in the same county.

Starting near each other, their paths diverged at first, to unite in due time in systematizing the most successful mode of training the youthful mind for the reception of the truths contained in the Holy Scriptures, of which the world has any knowledge.

The stones for the temple of Solomon were prepared

from designs drawn by a master hand; the work was so well done and the numbering so perfect, that upon uniting them in the building, all came to their appropriate places without the sound of any tool of iron being heard upon them.

When we see how admirably the different parts of the work by Raikes and Fox united to form a perfect edifice, who can doubt that they were workmen executing the designs of a MASTER hand, in building as it were a vestibule to the Church, and that the Sabbath School and Church were hereafter to be as the outer and inner gates to "that spiritual building, that house not made with hands, eternal in the heavens."

The name of Fox has long been associated with some of the purest divines and statesmen of England. America has especial cause to remember with gratitude the noble stand taken in our favor by one of that name in the English Parliament during our struggle for a national existence. But there was another of that name to whom not only America but all the world should feel grateful for his noble stand in favor of poor and down-trodden humanity.

William Fox, the subject of this Memoir, was born February 14, 1736, at the village of Clapton, a few miles northeast of the city of Gloucester, in Gloucestershire, England. I have been unable to procure anything like a satisfactory account of the genealogy of the ancestors of Mr. Fox in the male line. His immediate ancestors were agriculturists—his father farmed the ancient family estate near the village of Clapton.

Both his parents were active Christians—they were members of the Baptist church at another village near Clapton, called Bourton-on-the-water; the church was then under the pastoral care of the Rev. Benjamin Beddome, A. M.

The family consisted of father, mother, and eight children—William being the youngest. How many were sons and how many were daughters I know not—there were two sons besides William, if no more; their names were Samuel and Edward. The father died in 1739, when William was in his third year. Left with so large a family of young children, it is said Mrs. Fox felt the burden upon her to be very heavy, accustomed as she had always been to the counsels and assistance of the kindest of husbands.

But she did not shrink from the task. Being a woman of superior intellect, she nobly met the responsibility—and as evidence of her success the life of this son need only to be cited. He however relates other evidences of the esteem in which she was held by the people of the village. If advice or assistance was needed in cases of affliction, their usual expression was "go to Mrs. Fox."

When William was seven years of age, his eldest brother, who was a farmer in the town, found him employment by sending him into the fields to keep the birds from the corn.

When a man becomes eminent for any particular trait of character, it is not difficult to find that his childhood abounded in incidents pointing in that direction, although the same events would have been passed unnoticed had he remained in obscurity.

An incident is related in the life of William Fox to show that perseverance was a prominent element in his character. When he was about ten years old, still watching the birds in the fields of his brother, he sat down under a tree and wept bitterly. "All my brothers," said he to himself, "are well provided for—but there is no prospect whatever of a comfortable provision for me." At length he came to the following conclusion, or rather formed a resolution most extraordinary for a boy in his circumstances at such an age—and which would ordinarily be looked upon as a childish whim. Said he—"I will get into some profitable business, and will pursue it with industry and care until I have acquired sufficient property to purchase this farm of my brother's—nor will I be content until I possess as my own the whole of this village and the Lordship which belongs to it."

The most remarkable thing about the whole affair is, that he succeeded in about forty years after in carrying out his designs, although he doubtless many times lost sight of his object—but in the end he that had been the destitute orphan became lord of the manor of Clapton, and this without any aid from his ancestors, the law in England giving to the eldest son the estate of his father. His employment in the fields prevented him from getting an education, although he earnestly desired to obtain one, and greatly lamented that so many barriers interposed between him and his desired object.

The leisure which he occasionally had, he endeavored to turn to the best account at the village school—and when the other boys were engaged at play in the intervals of school hours, he was found diligently employed at his studies.

The following incident will serve to show the good opinion which his teacher had of his promising abilities and general good conduct. One of his teachers had a brother at Abingdon in Berkshire, who wanted an apprentice, and he selected William Fox as the most suitable for the situation—and although he was but ten years of age, this teacher recommended him to his brother. Anxious to get out into the world, not forgetting his dreams of becoming lord of the manor of Clapton, and having obtained the consent of his affectionate mother, William went to Abingdon and entered with ardor upon the duties of his new situation.

The work he was called upon to perform was soon found too laborious for him, so that at the end of six months he was compelled to relinquish his situation and return home, where he again resumed his employment on the farm, and continued to do so until his seventeenth year.

With the little education he had obtained, he, as many others have done at that time of life, made several attempts at poetry, and although he was not destined to become eminent as a poet, these efforts were not without their good effects—for one of his elder brothers happened to see a copy of some of his verses, and from the merit which they developed, he insisted that William should be placed if possible in a situation more suitable to his tastes and inclinations for improving his mind.

Failing in his efforts to place him in a school, this brother found means in the year 1752 to introduce him to Mr. R., a mercer and draper at Oxford, (one account says York was the place, but that is a mistake,) and this circumstance proved to be that event, or turning point which led, under the direction of the Supreme Being, to the accomplishment of his wishes.

Having begun to learn a trade later in life than was common in England, it would require more than ordinary exertions to become proficient in his business at the usual age. It has not been possible to obtain much information concerning his manner of life during his apprenticeship. What can be procured, however, establishes the fact that his conduct was unexceptionable, and might safely be adopted as a model for other young men in similar situations. To confirm this, it need only be stated that his employer soon placed him at the head of his business, and two years before the expiration of his apprenticeship, gave up to him his house and shop, with the stock of goods, amounting in value to between three and four thousand pounds— fifteen and twenty thousand dollars.

This act of his employer was the more remarkable from the fact, that he was a man whose parsimonious habits were proverbial—and besides, he had two nephews in his employment, both of whom were older and had been longer in business than the subject of this memoir. He and his employer differed widely in their ideas of doing business—the latter did not hesitate to do business on the Sabbath with any of his customers who were willing to desecrate the day; he was also in the habit of asking more for an article than he intended to take, rather than let his customer go.

When his employer proposed that he should take his business out of his hands, Mr. Fox told him explicitly that if he accepted his offer he should pursue quite a different course, as he was resolved neither to transact business on the Sabbath, nor ask one price for his goods and sell at another. The reply was—"Mr. Fox, if you do not serve on Sunday, you will very soon lose all the business."

But his acts gave the strongest evidence that ungodly men respect professing Christians when their deportment and business transactions are consistent with their profession, and that they prefer entrusting important affairs to their keeping rather than to one of their own number—for he still manifests his confidence in Mr. Fox by giving up the whole of his business above named, without demanding any other security than his business qualifications, industrious habits and correct moral deportment afforded.

For the encouragement of all young men, it is proper to say that so far from the prediction of his employer being fulfilled, Mr. Fox was so signally blessed in all his business transactions, that in a very few years he was enabled to pay off the whole amount of his indebtedness, and found himself in very comfortable circumstances, with an income more than sufficient to meet all demands against him, and a reputation as a business man unsullied.

His house and table were always ready for the reception of friends, and especially for the young theological students who were prosecuting their studies at the University.

The Rev. Dr. Hawies, who afterwards became famous for his efforts to promote religious and missionary enterprises, is said to have been a frequent visiter at his house about this time.

About a year before Mr. Fox entered into business, he and one of his sisters were baptized at Bourton-on-the-water, uniting with the church there—thus following the footsteps of their parents.

Mr. Fox attributes his conversion (under Providence) to the reading of the only religious book in the house of his employer, except the Bible. We are not informed what book that was.

Mr. Fox being a dissenter from some of the doctrines of the Established Church of England, could not consistently, as he thought, unite in communion with the members of that church, neither did he approve of their mode of conducting public worship ; but his religion was of that catholic spirit that would prefer to remove barriers to denominational intercourse, rather than build them up. He therefore attended the ministry of his friend, Dr. Hawies. After his settlement in business, the next important event of his history was to select a companion for life. His views on that subject, although they might not admit of universal application, would, if generally adopted, prevent many unhappy marriages. He used to say that there were three things in regard to marriage, he was resolved NOT to do—first, I will not marry a lady who is not decidedly pious ; second, I must be satisfied that I can respectably maintain her ; and third, I must have her father's consent.

To these resolutions he is said to have rigidly adhered—and about the year 1761 he was married to Miss Mary Tabor, eldest daughter of Jonathan Tabor, Esq., a merchant of Colchester, in the county of Essex—a gentleman very highly esteemed for his correct Christian deportment in all his dealings. In this conection Mr. and Mrs. Fox, during a period of more than sixty years, were unusually blessed in all the relations of life.

Not having the privilege of attending a church of his own order at Oxford, about the year 1764 he purchased a large business in Leadenhall street, London, and removed to that city.

Soon after his removal to London he united with the Baptist Church in Prescott street, Goodman's Fields, then under the care of the Rev. Samuel Buford, and in a short time under that of the Rev. Abraham Booth. He now enjoyed not only the advantages of Mr. Booth's edifying ministry, but his intimate acquaintance, together with that of a number of others who were eminent for their social and religious characteristics. These advantages afforded him much enjoyment, and were more highly prized in consequence of his having been to some extent deprived of them for a considerable time. One of these gentlemen was Joseph Gutteridge, Esq., of Denmark Hill, Camberwell.

A short time after Mr. Fox commenced business in London he met with many discouragements. The retail trade in which he was engaged did not meet his expectations—in addition to this, he had been there but a short time when he was attacked with a violent fever, which it was thought would terminate fatally. On this occasion his father-in-law, Mr. Tabor, visited him, and according to his establshed custom on all trying occasions, founded upon the teachings of the Scriptures, particularly of the fifth chapter of the general epistle of James, fourteenth and fifteenth verses, he requested some of the praying friends of Mr. Fox to assemble for the purpose of uniting in fervent supplication, if it was the Divine will and would be for the glory of God, that their afflicted brother might be restored to health.

It is said that while they were thus engaged, Mr. Tabor received such assurances that their prayers would be answered, that he said with great confidence at the close of the exercises, "Mr. Fox will live." As an evidence that his assurances were genuine, it need only be mentioned that Mr. Fox began immediately to recover, so that in a short time he was enabled to return to his business, which improved from that time forward—so that he not long afterwards removed to Cheapside and engaged in the wholesale trade, which also prospered in his hands, until he became quite wealthy, and was enabled to engage in various benevolent enterprises.

In reference to this period of his life, and especially in regard to the happiness he enjoyed in church fellowship, one of his children who survived him says,

"He was useful and respected at this time in no common degree; he in later years looked back upon that period of his life with regret, and called those his halcyon days."

The wholesale trade in which Mr. Fox had engaged made it necessary for him to take frequent journeys through the several counties or shires of England, which afforded him frequent opportunities of witnessing the deplorable ignorance of the poorer classes. He often found hamlets and even villages where the poor were entirely without the Bible—and what made this destitution still worse, he discovered that when they were presented with a copy, not one in twenty could read it.

This deplorable state of things gave him food for much serious reflection, and caused him to spend much time in devising means to remedy the evil.

The friends with whom he consulted gave him little encouragement, because they thought nothing short of legislation by Parliament could effect anything worth the trouble—there being no system of free schools in England. So Mr. Fox felt, and accordingly applied both personally and by letter to many of its leading members in both houses—but was compelled soon to relinquish all hope of getting assistance for such an object from the government.

It was about this time (1783 or '4) that Mr. Fox purchased the manor of Clapton in his native village;

thus accomplishing what he had resolved to do at ten years of age, while fighting the birds from his brother's corn.

This gave him an opportunity to commence his benevolent efforts in favor of education in his native place. His first step towards this object was to clothe comfortably all the poor people in the village—men, women and children. He next set up a week-day school for the free instruction of all who were willing to attend it. In this school the reading was confined to the Bible, and as there was no chapel in the village the children and all those who partook of his bounty, were directed to attend service on the Sabbath at the parish—(Episcopal)—church.

Mr. Fox had long been desirous, and had made known his wishes several years before to some of his friends, "that every poor person in the kingdom might be able to read the Bible," and in the most pressing manner recommended the establishment of a Society equal to the carrying out of such an object.

The magnitude of the undertaking seemed too great, and there was no one willing to take the lead—consequently Mr. Fox himself undertook the work, and at the Baptist Monthly Meeting held at the King's Head tavern in the Poultry, in May, 1785, introduced the subject, and submitted to their consideration the question whether there might not be some plan adopted by which all the children of the poor might receive a scriptural education by being taught to read the Bible.

The Chairman on this occasion was Henry Kane, Esq., of Walworth; he was a deacon in the Baptist church at Mazepond, of which the Rev. James Dove was pastor. Mr. Fox introduced his subject by the following address—

"Mr. Chairman—Unaccustomed to speak in public, and but little acquainted with the mode of conducting public business, I rise with peculiar diffidence to bring before you a subject which, though unconnected with that for which we are assembled, and consequently not within our notice as a committee, will I trust, be found worthy of your consideration as gentlemen and as Christians.

"And while I feel and lament my own inability for so important a work, and sincerely wish it were in more able hands, it will not, I trust, be necessary to plead like an Apollos a cause already countenanced by some of the gentlemen present, and which I hope will find the most powerful advocate in the generous breasts of all; for generosity, though not confined to this country, or peculiar to this city, is however one of its leading characters—nor has it anywhere shone with greater lustre than in the circle with which I am now surrounded.

"Animated with these sentiments, and feeling as I

do the most disinterested concern for the poor, I wish to place them under your protection, where, cherished by your influence, this little plantation, hitherto neglected except by the fostering care of a few individuals, might rise into a forest and fill the country.—Who that passes through the villages can view with unconcern the toil of tho laborer, while he reflects upon the trifling pittance it affords him! For several months in the year he does not receive more than five or six shillings a week—and on these slender earnings exist (and it is but an existence) the whole family.

"Enter his cottage, and you will see the indigent pair dealing out to their children their scanty allowance; bread and water are frequently all their fare, and it would pierce a heart of stone to hear them crying for more, which their wretched parents are unable to give. Their clothing also bears the mark of extreme indigence; a few rags are thrown over the shoulders of some, while others are almost in a state of nature. A little straw serves them for a bed—where the rain trickling from the thatch, and the piercing wind whistling through the time-worn cottage, interrupt their repose, and prevent their losing the remembrance of their sorrows in the arms of sleep.

"This is not an exaggerated or a solitary instance, but what may too often be found both in our towns and villages. Great however as the temporal evils of the poor are, and numerous as their wants appear, for these I ask no relief;* but I do ask, nay, I entreat your aid for the support of schools, that while the poor remain destitute of the comforts of this life, they may not be altogether unacquainted with that which is to come. Could it have been imagined that in a Christian country—a Protestant country too—no provision would be made for the education of poor children, about which the heathen took so much pains. So however it is—and it is a shame to the Christian name.

"Without a Bible in their houses—and if they had one, without ability to read it—too much neglected by the clergy as well as deserted by others, the poor live as the beasts that perish. What an opportunity then is here of displaying that generosity for which the heathen were so renowed—and of which permit me to remind you of a single example.

"When Xerxes entered Greece at the head of nearly three millions of men, he was encountered at the pass of Thermopylæ, by Leonidas, king of Sparta, who only had four thousand. Victory, from local situation and the peculiar circumstances under which the Grecians fought, would in all probability have long re-

* Mr. Fox certainly would desire to see their temporal wants relieved, otherwise he would not have clothed all the poor in his native village, but he is now however asking for relief of another kind.

mained in suspense, had they not been betrayed and almost surrounded.

"In this critical moment Leonidas dismissed all his soldiers except three hundred Spartans, with whom, determined to conquer or die, he defended the pass—till after laying twenty thousand of the enemy dead at his feet, himself and his companions were slain also.

"This victory opened to Xerxes a passage to the very gates of Athens. The Athenians, wisely judging it impossible to hold out against so powerful a host, resolved to quit their city and retire to their ships—but before they put in practice this desperate resolution, they determined to send their old men, women and children to Freyene, a city at some distance, bordering on the sea—the citizens of which, notwithstanding the extreme danger to which they also were exposed, received them cordially, maintained them at the public expense—and, as though maintenance and education were inseparably connected, established at the same time a fund for the support of these strangers, and schools for the education of their children. To have been a citizen of that city, sir, under the circumstances just related, would have reflected an honor upon you and upon me, to which the wealth of a Crœsus, the power of a Xerxes, or the conquests of an Alexander would never have raised us.

"Had the old men, women and children of a strange city or country requested under similar circumstances an asylum with us, should we have received and supported them? I trust we should. Should we have *educated* the children of these strangers also? Should we, I ask, have extended our benevolent regards to the education of their children? Perhaps we might; and I venture to hope that we should. Let us, however, no longer delay to follow their example with respect to our own. Consider the children of the poor as looking up to us and asking, not for the supply of their material wants, but for the means of instruction only. And shall Christians deny to their own children that which heathens granted the children of strangers?

"There is not perhaps, sir, a more acceptable service rendered to our Divine Lord than that of training the children in the way in which they should go. Let us appropriate a little of that money which the Jews expended in travelling to Jerusalem to worship, and a little of that time which the primitive Christians spent in wandering from city to city and from country to country, and let us devote it to the children of the poor.

* * * * *

"Let none of my friends be alarmed at the magnitude of the undertaking, and conclude because it is not in our power to furnish bread for a thousand persons perishing with hunger, therefore we will relieve none of them. Who is there amongst us but knows that some of the most important events have taken their rise from very trifling beginnings. Witness the 'Society for Promoting Religious Knowledge among the Poor.' Two friends I have understood said one to the other, 'What shall we do to promote the glory of God, and the good of mankind?' The reply was 'Let us purchase a few books and give to the poor.' A trifle —not more than eight shillings—was subscribed for that purpose ; and it need not be told this respectable meeting, many of whom are the worthy supporters of it, by what hasty strides this excellent charity has advanced to its present greatness.

"Suffice it to say there is but one thing wanting to make it one of the most benevolent institutions that has yet been established. You will readily perceive the one thing to which I allude is that now submitted to your consideration—for of what use are Bibles to those who cannot read them ?

"It would ill become me to dictate to this assembly what kind of plan they ought to adopt—but were I asked the question, I should say—Fix on a spot where some lively, zealous gospel minister resides, and in his village and those in his neighborhood establish schools. These he might visit without much inconvenience, and in catechising the children he might also in a plain and simple way introduce the Gospel among the parents."

Thus we have in the above address of Mr. Fox, the commencement of that discussion which led to the formation of the first Sunday School Society, although the idea of Sunday Schools had not at that time entered his mind.

Every one must be astonished at the thought of doing by voluntary contributions that which not more than half of our States have been able to do by land appropriations and taxation.

We have reason, however, to believe that Mr. Fox's plan was not deemed chimerical by those present from the fact, that measures were immediately taken to raise a committee—and it was agreed that a meeting should be called to take the matter into serious consideration. A subscription was commenced at once for carrying it into effect.

The Chairman of that meeting, Mr. Henry Kane, said to Mr. Fox, " I presume, sir, you intend to confine the plan to our own denomination, for then we shall go on in harmony."

Mr. Fox replied—" Sir, the work is great, and I shall not be satisfied until every person in the world be able to r ead the Bible—and therefore we must call on all the world to help us."

The proposed public meeting was fixed for August 16th, at the same place, the King's Head Tavern in the Poultry. The following address for convening the meeting was prepared by the Provisional Committee, (most probably by Mr. Fox himself, as he was always one of the most active members of every committee,) and sent to the clergy and leading citizens of the city of London.

"*To the Benevolent and Humane in favor of the Illiterate Poor :*

"You cannot be entirely unacquainted with that extreme ignorance in which multitudes of poor persons, even in this land of Gospel light, exist—raised but a small degree above the brute creation, unable to read the Bible, and incapable of procuring an acquaintance with it. There is no reason to wonder, therefore, if they discover a spirit hostile to Christianity, and indulge dispositions that are the bane of civil society ; evils these, over which the wise and good have ever mourned, and against the growing effects of which many laudable attempts have been made by benevolent individuals with obvious success.

"Nothing has contributed so much towards promoting this design as early instruction ; for that the soul be without knowledge is not good. Schools are already established in various parts of the country, in which the poor of different ages are taught to read.

"But as these establishments have been much circumscribed, it is the wish of many individuals in the metropolis, who have already entered into subscription, that a design, in their apprehension of the greatest importance to the community at large and to the poor in particular, should become general.

"In this good work all the benevolent and humane are earnestly entreated to unite, for, were they to enter the villages that are remote from the rich and the great, they would find them exhibit in striking colors the necessity of such a charitable exertion; the sad scenes of poverty and ignorance there beheld would be appeals too powerful for a compassionate mind to resist. Who then that possesses an ability but would rejoice in an opportunity of diffusing the light of divine knowledge amongst persons that are enveloped with darkness, and that would not endeavor to dispel from their minds that worst of all evils, ignorance of themselves and of the true character of the God that made them?

"With a view to the forming of a permanent Society for the benevolent purpose and on the most catholic plan, a meeting will be held at the King's Head Tavern in the Poultry, on Tuesday, the 16th of August, at five o'clock in the afternoon, at which time and place it is requested that all such gentlemen as wish well to the design will give their attendance.

"London, July 26, 1785."

A short time after the meeting in May, at which Mr. Fox proposed the design of forming a society, his attention was called to the fact that Robert Raikes, Esq., a gentleman who was the Editor and Publisher of a paper called the "Gloucester Journal," had published an article with regard to Sabbath Schools in his paper of Nov. 3, 1783, and that Colonel Townley, of Lancashire, had written to the Mayor of Gloucester for more information concerning them; that the Mayor had handed the letter to Mr. Raikes, who answered it, giving a full statement of their origin and the manner of conducting them, a copy of that letter—which may be found in the preceding chapter—having been published in the London papers, Mr. Fox had an opportunity of perusing it. He at once saw how superior this plan of Sunday Schools was to his own plan of week-day schools, provided they would accomplish the object in view.

Being a member and Chairman of the Provisional Committee that had been appointed by the first meeting "to prepare a plan for a Society to promote universal education among the poor," he immediately opened a correspondence with Mr. Raikes upon that subject, although they were previously unknown to each other. That correspondence will be introduced in the succeeding chapters, for the twofold purpose of biography and history.

CHAPTER IV.

THE following letter from Mr. Fox is the beginning of a correspondence between him and Mr. Raikes, which continued with many personal interviews to the end of their lives.

LONDON, June 15, 1785.

SIR—The liberality and goodness of heart manifested in your benevolent plan of Sunday Schools, I trust, render unnecessary any apology though from a stranger, when it is considered that his only view in writing is that he may be enabled to copy after so worthy an example.

You must know, sir, long before your excellent letter appeared in the papers, I had a compassion, and entertained sentiments for the indigent and ignorant poor extremely similar to your own. This led me to set up a school in one of our villages, (Clapton, near Bourton-on-the-water,) but as it is a daily one, and therefore attended with far greater expense, and perhaps with less utility than yours, it will very much oblige me, and probably greatly promote the design I have in view, if you will please to favor me with a further account of your plan, if any alteration, and what particular advantages have resulted from it since the publication of your letter. I have been apprehensive, and shall be extremely glad to find myself mistaken, that it would be difficult, if not impossible, to teach children to read by their attendance on schools only one day in seven. This is very material for me to know; and if they can, it will also be as desirable to ascertain the average time it takes for such instruction, together with the age at which they are taken, the mode pursued by the teachers, and the expense attending the same.

The reason I am thus particular is because a society is forming in town, to which I belong, for carrying a plan of this sort into general use. The design, I dare say, will appear to you laudable, but at the same time difficult. Its success depends on the concurrence and aid of well-disposed Christians throughout the kingdom. Great events, however, having frequently taken their rise from small, and, to human appearance, trifling beginnings.

We wish to make a trial; and as the committee for drawing up a plan meet on the 23rd instant, I beg the favor of your reply prior to that time, that we may have the benefit of an experienced work, in order to assist in our deliberation.

I remain, Sir,

Yours, &c.,

W. Fox.

To R. Raikes, Esq., Gloucester.

To this letter Mr. Raikes wrote the following reply, dated

Gloucester, June 20, 1785.

Sir—You may justly suppose that an apology was utterly unnecessary for a letter like yours. I am full of admiration at the great, the noble design you speak of as forming. If it were possible that my poor abilities could be rendered in any degree useful to you, point out the object, and you will find me not inactive.

Allow me to refer you to a letter I wrote about a week ago, to Jonas Hanway, Esq., upon the subject of Sunday Schools; if you ask him for a sight of it, I dare say he will send it to you.

With respect to the possibility of teaching children by the attendance they give upon the Sunday, I thought with you, at my first onset, that little was to be gained; but I now find that it has suggested to the parents that the little progress we made on the Sunday might be improved, and they have therefore engaged to give the teachers a penny a week to admit the children once or twice a day during the recess from work, at dinner time or evening, to take a lesson every day in the week.

To one of my teachers who lives in the worst part of our suburbs, I allow two shillings a week extra, (besides the shilling I give for the Sunday employ) to let all that are willing come and read in this manner; I see admirable effects from this addition to my scheme. I find mothers of the children and grown up young women have begged to be admitted to partake of this benefit. Sorry I am to say that none of the other sex have shown the same desire.

A clergyman from Painswick called on me this afternoon, and expressed his surprise at the progress made there. Many boys now can read, who certainly have no other opportunity than what they derive from their Sunday instruction. This he assured me was the fact. I hear the people of the Forest of Dean have begun to set this machine in motion among the children of the colliers, a most savage race. A person from Mitchel Dean called upon me a few days ago to report their progress. "Sir," said he, "we have many children now who, three months ago, knew not a letter from a cart-wheel, (that was his expression) who can now repeat hymns in a manner that would astonish you."

I have been out of town, or should have answered your polite letter sooner; I now have only time to give you these facts. When you have seen my letter to Mr. Hanway you will be able to judge whether further use can be made of the little experience I have had, in this attempt at civilization. I can only say, show wherein I may be useful, and command without reserve.

Your obedient servant,

R. Raikes.

It will be noticed how heartily Mr. Raikes endorses the project of forming a society "full of admiration at the great, the noble design you speak of as forming," no jarring or jealousy here, but an honest recognition of a co-worker in carrying out the grand design drawn by Him who is above all. We have no means of ascertaining the contents of his letter to Mr. Hanway, but we have doubtless the substance of it in his other letters.

The next meeting according to the proposal in the circular of the Provisional Committee, was held on the 16th of August and was very respectably attended. Mr. Thomas Hunt was called to the chair. It appeared, however, that no one present was prepared to deliver his sentiments on the subject for which the assembly was convened, and Mr. Fox being called upon reported to the assembly his correspondence with Mr. Raikes since their former meeting, and recommended that they proceed with the organization of their society, but that instead of the original plan proposed, it be a society for promoting *Sunday Schools*

This suggestion meeting with general approbation, a committee of fourteen gentlemen was chosen to take measures for carying it into effect. Mr. Fox being the original mover of the whole design, he was, of course, a member of the committee. He was requested by the other members to prepare a circular letter, and send it to various persons of influence, for the purpose of obtaining a more general meeting on the 30th of the same month at the Paul's Head Tavern, Cateaton street.

The following is a copy of the circular :—

FRIDAY, Aug 26, 1785.

SIR—Encouraged by the promising success of the Sunday Schools established in some towns and villages of this kingdom, several gentlemen met on Tuesday evening, the 16th inst., at the King's Head Tavern in the Poultry, to consider of the utility of forming a society for the establishment and support of Sunday Schools throughout the kingdom of Great Britain.

At this meeting it was agreed to form such a society, and a committee of fourteen gentlemen were chosen to draw up a code of laws for the government of the said society, and a set of proper rules for the regulation of the schools.

The committee having met and drawn up a plan for

the intended society, and the laws and rules necessary for it, and the schools, they propose to submit their plan to the consideration of all such gentlemen as shall attend a public meeting, to be holden on Tuesday next, the 30th inst., at the Paul's Head Tavern, Cateaton street, at four o'clock in the afternoon.

To prevent vice, to encourage industry and virtue, to dispel the darkness of ignorance, to diffuse the light of knowledge, to bring men cheerfully to submit to their stations—to obey the laws of God and their country, to make that useful part of the community the country poor happy, to lead them in the pleasant paths of religion here, and to endeavor to prepare them for a glorious eternity, are the objects proposed by the promoters of this institution.

To effect these great, these noble ends, they hope to form a society which will be enabled to establish Sunday Schools on a plan so extensive as to reach the remotest part of this island, and they flatter themselves they shall receive the support, assistance, and patronage of persons of every rank and description.

Private advantage and party zeal are entirely disclaimed by the friends and promoters of this laudable institution. However men may be divided into political parties, or however Christians may unhappily separate from each other on account of difference of sentiment, here they are all invited to join in the common cause, the glory of God, the good of their country and the happiness of their fellow-creatures.

Permit me to request the favor of your attendance at the proposed meeting.

I am, sir, by order of the committee,

Your humble servant,

William Fox.

A copy of this circular was sent to Thomas Raikes, Esq., a banker in London; he transmitted it to his brother Robert, at Gloucester, who, upon receiving it, addressed the following reply to Mr. Fox:

Gloucester, Monday, Aug. 29, 1785.

Dear Sir—My brother, Thomas Raikes, enclosed to me yesterday, a circular letter he had received with your signature, which has given me more pleasure than I can express. I observe by that letter you have a meeting to-morrow. I regret that I am not situated near enough to attend it, but as I was present yesterday se'night [seven night or one week] at a meeting which is intended to be established as an anniversary, at Mitchel Dean, a little town in this county on the verge of the Forrest of Dean, it occurred to me that a sketch of the pleasing scene I there beheld may not be improperly laid before the gentlemen who attend your summons to the Paul's Head Tavern.

Maynard Colchester, and William Lane, Esqs., two gentlemen of property in the neighborhood, having heard of the happy effects arising from an attention to the morals of the rising generation of the poor, determined to try what could be done among the little lawless rabble which inhabit the borders of the Forest near Mitchel Dean.

About Christmas last, they established two schools, and admittted fifty or sixty scholars of both sexes, some of them the most uncivilized beings in the country. Ten or twelve of the respectable inhabitants of the town engaged to subscribe, but what was of greater moment, they took upon themselves the superintendence of the establishment; and to their zeal may be ascribed under the Divine blessing, its success. The promoters of the undertaking did me the honor to invite me to dine with them on their anniversary, to witness the progress that has been made in this effort at civilization. The children, though many of them in apparel very ragged, were extremely clean. They walked in great order, two and two, to the church, where they were placed in the gallery, exposed to the view of the whole congregation; and their behavior during the service was perfectly silent and becoming. In the repetition of the Lord's Prayer they all joined, and formed a charm that made every heart dilate with joy. The clergyman of the parish, a curate of £26, ($130) a year, gave an admirable discourse from Mark iv. 28. This valuable young man had taken great pains in admonishing the children, and impressing them with due notions, how greatly their own happiness would be increased, by introducing into their behavior habits of quietness and good nature to one another. The tenor of argument in his discourse was to prove that if good seed be sown in the moral, as in the natural world, a plentiful harvest was no less to be hoped for, but that we must look for it in the same order; it might be some time before it made its appearance, and then by small beginnings; first the blade, &c.

After church, the children were conducted to the inn, where an examination took place of the progress made in reading. I was highly pleased to see the proficiency some of them had made. Several could read in the Testament; and I found among them two or three with extraordinary memories. They have learned to repeat several chapters.

Near fifty of them were perfect in their Catechism, and all could repeat some of Dr. Watts' Hymns. The children were so much pleased with those pieces, that two or three of them could repeat the whole book. But what pleased me most of all, was the result of my inquiry into the effect upon their manners. "That boy," said one of the gentlemen, (pointing to a very ill-looking lad about 13,) "was the most profligated little dog in this neighborhood. He was the leader of every kind of mischief and wickedness. He never opened his lips without a profane or indecent expression. And now he has become orderly and good-natured, and in his conversation has quite left off profaneness."

After dinner, the gentlemen called in six boys, who had previously been taught a hymn, which I assure you they sang to admiration. I observed that one of the singers was the boy before mentioned. The silence that prevailed among the children was very remarkable; their benefactors dined in a room adjoining, but were not disturbed with their talking.

I have given you this little recital, and if it tends to prove the practability of doing good to our fellow-creatures, I hope it may prove an incitement to the work you are bringing forward.

I am, with great respect, Sir,
Your most obedient servant,
R. Raikes.

To William Fox, Esq., Cheapside, London.

On the 30th of August, the third meeting was held, and Jonas Hanway, to whom Mr. Raikes's first letter introduced Mr. Fox, was called upon to preside. The following are the minutes:

At a meeting held at the Paul's Head Tavern, Cateaton street, this evening, the 30th of August, 1785, for the purpose of taking into consideration the propriety of establishing and supporting Sunday Schools for the instruction of poor children in different parts of the kingdom, Jonas Hanway, Esq., in the chair,

Resolved, unanimously, That it is the opinion of this meeting, that great benefit would accrue to the community at large from the adoption of such a measure, and that a society be formed for carrying the same into immediate effect.

Resolved, unanimously, That a general meeting be held at the Paul's Head Tavern, Cateaton street, on Wednesday, the 7th of September, at four o'clock, P. M., where the company of all those gentlemen who are friends to the undertaking is particularly requested.

Resolved unanimously, That the thanks of this meeting be given to those gentlemen who have been the means of bringing forward this laudable design.

Resolved unanimously, That the thanks of this meeting be given to the Chairman.

Resolved unanimously, That these resolutions be published in the London papers.

The following letter from Mr. Fox to Mr. Raikes contains a more full account of the last mentioned meeting.

LONDON, Sept. 2, 1785.

Dear Sir—The favor you did me by your kind letter of the 29th ult. was more than you can possibly conceive. This letter, together with extracts I made from some of your other letters, was read, and afforded much useful information. Presuming upon the friendship with which you honored me, and particularly encouraged by your last favor, I took the liberty of waiting on your brother, the bank director, to request his acceptance of the Chair, well knowing how much depended on such a choice. Both your brothers received me with politeness and cordiality—promised the design countenance and support—but declined the Chair, as the bank director was just going out of town. They then advised me to go to Mr. Thornton, another bank director—and your elder brother accompanied me to him. He also made the same kind offer of support, &c. which your brothers had done, but was unfortunately going out of town likewise, and advised me to apply to Mr. Hanway, who took the Chair soon after five o'clock.

The report of the Committee was read over, but not fully entered into, because the meeting was called by circular letters to the clergy, magistrates, and principal inhabitants, and not advertised in the public papers. The business, therefore, is put off till next Wednesday, when another meeting will be called by public advertisement, to be at the same place and time [of day] as the last.

Should anything occur which you think likely to forward the important design, your communicating the same will confer the greatest obligation on, dear sir, your much obliged friend and humble servant,

WM. FOX.

To R. RAIKES, Esq., Gloucester.

N. B. The fire which you had the honor to light up in Gloucester, having now reached the metropolis, will, I trust, never be extinguished but with the ignorance of every individual throughout the kingdom.

Some copies of the above letter having been published without the postscript, I have been the more particular to insert it here, because it has been erroneously stated that Mr. Fox claimed the honor of having established Sunday Schools without the knowledge of Mr. Raikes' efforts in the same direction—that postscript disproves any such assertion.

The fourth meeting was held according to appoint ment on the seventh of September, for the purpose of carrying the former resolution to organize a society for establishing and supporting Sunday Schools into execution.

Jonas Hanway was again called to the Chair. At this meeting it was resolved unanimously that a society be now established in London for the support and encouragement of Sunday Schools in the different counties of England; which Committee was then and there organized, but we are not informed of the exact manner in which it was done. A new Committee was chosen, consisting of twenty-four gentlemen instead of fourteen, as before—and it was agreed, in order to prevent the idea that there was any denominational spirit in the movement, that one half of them should be members of the Protestant Episcopal Church, and the remainder of Protestant dissenters. A resolution was then passed that the new Committee be directed to prepare a plan for the regulation of the Society, and present the same at the next general meeting. Another resolution was passed appointing seven of the principal bankers of the city to receive subscriptions for the support of the Society.

Thus it will be seen the *First Sunday School Society ever known was organized in the city of London on the seventh day of September, A.D.* 1785.

It afterwards settled upon the name of "THE SOCIETY FOR PROMOTING SUNDAY SCHOOLS THROUGHOUT THE BRITISH DOMINIONS," which previous to the organization of any other Society, was abbreviated into "The Sunday School Society." It would be most appropriate now to speak of it as "the First Sunday School Society." Every nation has some one of the three hundred and sixty-five days of each year, the annual return of which is celebrated by them in memory of their organization, or some other event in their history. Many of the religious denominations and other institutions have the same.

The organization of Sunday Schools would be an appropriate event to celebrate—but of that we do not know the exact date—not even the year ; it was 1781 or '2, we know not which. The birthday of Raikes or Fox would also be an appropriate event to celebrate, but to notice one and not the other would be only half doing the work. The organization of that Society, however, is without a rival, as the climax to which the labors of both contributed, providing not only for local advantages, but for diffusing Sabbath School influences throughout the British dominions, and eventually throughout the world.

Therefore there is no event connected with any nation, church, or any other institution, that it would be so universally appropriate to celebrate in all parts of the world, and by all denominations of Christians, as this—it comes at a season of year when the fruits of the earth, especially in Europe and North America, are most abundant ; and as picnics and excursions have become almost a rule with Sabbath Schools, we would respectfully suggest that in future all Sabbath Schools select the seventh of September when practicable for their celebrations. They can, by so doing make them serve the double purpose of a gala day, and a commemoration of the most important event in their history.

They will also hand down the names of Robert

Raikes and William Fox as noble examples of genuine philanthropy, who were willing to lay aside their denominational peculiarities, and unite their efforts for the glory of God and the good of mankind.

CHAPTER V.

IMMEDIATELY after the organization of the Society, the annexed Circular was published for general distribution—

SIR—The deplorable ignorance of the children of the poor in many parts of this kingdom, and the corruption of morals frequently flowing from that source, have long been matter of deep concern to all who are solicitous for the welfare of their country.

In manufacturing towns where children from their infancy are necessarily employed the whole week, no opp ortunity occurs for their receiving the least degree of education. To remedy this evil, some gen tlemen, actuated by the most benevolent motives have established in some of these towns Sunday Schools, where children and others are taught to read, and are instructed in the knowledge of their duty as rational beings. The Sunday too often spent by the children of the poor in idleness and play, or in contracting habits of vice and dissipation, is by the child ren of these schools employed in learning to read the Bible, and in attending the public worship of God, by which means they are trained up in habits of virtue and piety, as well as industry, and a foundation is laid for their becoming useful members of the community.

The numerous benefits arising from Sunday Schools of which the most indubitable testimonies have been given, and the great importance of extending their salutary effects, have induced a number of gentlemen, stimulated by the successful attempts, to establish a Society in London for the support and encouragement of Sunday Schools in the different counties of England.

The Committee for conducting the affairs of this Society, anxious to extend the beneficial influence of these schools as speedily as possible, have taken the liberty of addressing you, sir, on this occasion; and of requesting you to communicate to such of the inhabitants of [your place] as may be disposed to encourage such an undertaking, the wish of the Committee to establish a Sunday School in that [town.] For more particular information they beg leave to refer you to the printed plan, copies of which are sent herewith to be distributed at your discretion; and an early intimation of the result of your proceedings will be highly acceptable to them.

It is the intention of this Society, on application being made to the Committee from any place, to assist in establishing a school or schools therein, until the good consequences shall be so apparent to the inhabitants as to encourage an exertion which may render any further assistance from the Society unnecessary.

In forming the plan of this Society, the most liberal and catholic principles have been adopted, in hopes that persons of all denominations of the Protestant faith will be induced to unite in carrying it into execution with greater energy. The Committee therefore beg leave to recommend to every minister of a congregation where these schools may be established, to make it known to the people of their respective charges, and to preach a collection sermon for the support of such schools as often as occasion may require.

If any further argument in favor of these schools was necessary, a striking one presents itself in the contemplation of our crowded prisons and frequent executions, which shock the feelings of humanity, and disgrace our country. The sad history of these wretched victims, to their crimes and to the laws, too plainly evinces that to the want of an early introduction into the paths of virtue and religion, to which this institution would lead, may be attributed, in a great degree, their unhappy end. In this point of view, then, this institution may be considered a political as well as a religious one, claiming the attention of those even who, if not particularly zealous in the cause of Christianity, cannot be insensible to the advantages that would accrue to society from the preservation of good order and the security of persons and property.

The Committtee flatter themselves they shall find in you a friend to this cause, and that your exertions, in union with theirs, will be crowned with success, in producing a reformation of morals in the lower ranks of the rising generation.

By order of the Committee.

Henry Thornton, Chairman.

Another general meeting was held on the 21st. of September following—Henry Thornton, Esq. again occupying the Chair. After having listened to the reading of the plan as reported by the Committee appointed for that purpose, the following resolutions were adopted—

Resolved, That the plan now produced by the Committee of the Society for the Support and Encouragement of Sunday Schools, be approved by this meeting.

Resolved, That the twenty-four gentlemen appointed a Committee at the last meeting do prepare the plan for publication, and take such other means for promoting the ends of this institution as may appear to them necessary, and report their proceedings to the next general meeting.

In reporting their plan the Committee prefaced it by some very lengthy remarks. They say that although there are numerous institutions of charity which are extant in the nation, there are still many distresses and wants unrelieved. They also say they are not so sanguine of the success of their plans as to suppose that ignorance, wretchedness and suffering can be wholly extirpated—that they know to be impossible while human nature remains unchanged—but they urge that while the inequality which exists from the nature and constitution of things, prevails in the world, the poor must be allowed their humble claim on the generosity of the rich.

They rejoice that the same providential hand that permitted the existence of evil, has implanted in the human breast a principle of benevolence to restrain and alleviate it.

They regret that in consideration of the numerous and extensive manufactories, and the extreme poverty of the operatives, parents are under the necessity of calling the services of their children into requisition as soon as their labor can be of any value. They are thus prevented from getting instruction at the proper age, and grow up in ignorance—this with poverty being their only inheritance from one generation to another.

Sabbath Schools in their opinion being the only or most effectual means of enabling them to know what the Scriptures contain, and reform them in morals and manners, to encourage those whom God has entrusted with wealth to contribute a portion of it to their support, they cite many instances of their good effects where they have already been established.

The Committee congratulate themselves and their country that they live in an age in which the denominational animosities of former times are not indulged in, but that professors of Christianity are more liberal in the construction of each other's motives, and are showing a willingness to go hand in hand to promote its true principles without bias from party prejudices.

The following are the rules and regulations of the Sunday School Society—

1. This Society shall consist of a President, four Vice-Presidents, a Treasurer, and all the governors, [directors.]

2. Subscriptions of one guinea, (equal to four dollars and sixty-six cents American money) per annum, shall constitute the subscriber governor during the continuance of his subscription.

3. A donation of ten guineas or upwards at one time or within one year, shall constitute the donor a governor for life, and all contributions, however small, will be gratefully accepted.

4. A general meeting shall be held on the second Wednesday of January, April, July and October, in each year, at which meetings seven governors shall constitute a Board.

5. The President, Vice-President, or Treasurer, or any of the Committee, shall have power to call a general meeting, giving one week's notice in the public papers.

6. A Committee of twenty-four, to consist equally of members of the Church of England and Protestant dissenters, shall be annually chosen from among the governors at the general meeting in January, who shall meet on the last Wednesday in every month for conducting the affairs of this Society. The President, Vice-President and Treasurer, shall be members of all committees ; and five members shall constitute a quorum.

7. A President, Vice-President, Treasurer or Secretary, when a vacancy happens by death or resignation, shall be proposed by the Committee for the approbation of the general meeting.

8. No governor shall vote at a general meeting for any appointment to this charity after the first year, who has not been a governor for twelve calendar months.

9. The Treasurer shall not pay any bills on account of this charity without an order signed by three of the Committee.

10. Five auditors shall be appointed by the general meeting to examine the bills and accounts of the Treasurer.

11. An account of the receipts and disbursements of this charity shall be annually published for the inspection of the governors.

12. The Secretary shall personally attend all the meetings of this charity unless prevented by indisposition, in which case he is to send a deputy. He shall keep an accurate and methodical account of the proceedings, and do all the incidental business of this charity. He shall apply for the annual subscription in London and its vicinity, and produce two or more securities to be approved by the monthly committee, who shall be bound with him in the amount of five hundred pounds, in one or more bonds. He shall pay all the subscriptions to the Treasurer or banker, and produce his account to the Committee every month—and not retain the amount of one hundred pounds at any time in his possession.

13. In all places where the Schools of the Society may be established, gentlemen of respectable character in the neighborhood shall be requested to visit them every Sunday, receive subscriptions, correspond with the Society, and suggest any improvement in the plan they may think necessary.

14. The Society shall provide Bibles and Testaments, and spelling-books for the use of the schools.

15. The Committee shall be at liberty to order lessons on week-days where they shall think necessary.

16. All the scholars shall attend some place of worship every Sunday, but such as their parents respectively approve.

I was inclined to leave out the set of rules above given, but could not see that I could give a clear understanding of the history of the Society's workings without it—besides the reading of those last three rules will pay for the time spent on all. In the fourteenth will be seen the first provision ever made for furnishing schools with books, and what the character of those books was.

By the fifteenth, we see there must have been a Hibernian element in the Society—they would not otherwise have provided for having Sunday Schools on *week-days*.

The sixteenth is a very important one, and with all our advantages for improvement, our hands have gone backward on that dial—children are not required to attend the regular services of the church as they should be. Parents professing to be Christians are very much to blame for this—a reform should begin at once.

The following rules were adopted by the Society for the government of individual schools. Such rules are not necessary now, but then they were all important—

when everything had to be learned by teachers and pupils.

1. The subjects of this charity shall be poor persons of each sex and any age, who shall be taught to read, at such times and in such places as the Committee, by themselves or their correspondents, shall appoint.

2. The teachers, by direction of the Committee or their correspondents, shall oblige all who are committed to their charge to attend public worship every Sunday, unless prevented by illness or any other sufficient cause.

3. The teachers shall take care that the scholars come clean to their respective schools—and if any scholars be guilty of lying, swearing, pilfering, talking in an indecent manner, or otherwise misbehaving themselves, the teacher shall point out the evil of such conduct; and if after repeated reproof the scholar shall not be reformed, he or she shall be excluded from the school.

4. The religious observation of the Christian Sabbath being an essential object with the Society for the Support and Encouragement of Sunday Schools, the exercise of the scholars on that day shall be restricted to reading in the Old and New Testament, and to spelling as a preparative for it.

5. A printed copy of the above rules shall be put

up in the schoolroom, and read by the teachers to the scholars the first Sunday in every month.

By the first rule we see that the schools were intended exclusively for the poor. It is difficult for us in America to understand why such a distinction was made. We can scarcely tell when we see a child in Sabbath School, whether its parents are rich or poor, for all dress so nearly alike that the poor are as likely to be clothed best as the rich—but in England, at that time, the children of the rich and poor could be distinguished at a glance—the rich were very rich, and the poor very poor.

The condition of the poor in England is very much improved since that time—the Sabbath Schools have made them more virtuous and intelligent, manufacturing has been and is being done more by machinery—thus cheapening all articles for the poor as well as the rich, and this too without reducing their pay; opportunities for the poor to emigrate from England to America, Australia and other countries, leaves much better employment for those that remain.

The second, third, and fourth rules relate almost exclusively to the religious training of the schools, and it is gratifying to see how nearly right they started—but in place of improving on them, we have scarcely held our own.

The first set of officers for the Society were elected

at a meeting held on the 12th of October, 1785, as follows—

President, the Right Hon. James, Earl of Salisbury; Vice-Presidents, Thomas Boddington, Esq., John Harmon, Esq., James Martin, Esq., M. P., Brook Watson, Esq., M. P. and Alderman; Treasurer, Henry Thornton, M. P.; Secretary, Mr. William Jacobson.

For the purpose of enlisting the ministers of religion in the good cause, both of the Established Church and of the various denominations of dissenters, the following circular was widely distributed in London and its vicinity, and also sent to different parts of the country. This may seem strange now, when all ministers of every denomination labor for the Sabbath School—but at that time there were those who stoutly opposed it, as we shall show before closing this volume.

LONDON, January 3, 1786.

Rev. Sir—The beneficial effects of the establishment of Sunday Schools in various parts of the island, have induced some gentlemen to form a Society in London for the purpose of promoting their extension. Of the objects of this institution and of the means proposed for their attainment, you will be more particularly informed by the printed plan now circulating—a copy of which we take the liberty of enclosing.

You will perceive, sir, that a reformation of manners amongst the lower orders of the people, is the aim of this institution; by endeavoring to rescue the youth more especially from the evil tendencies of idle and dissipated habits and examples—to excite an attention to moral obligations, and to administer some instruction on the principles of the Christian religion—advantages from which multitudes of our fellow creatures are excluded by the indigence or profligacy of their parents or other connections; these causes operating in a melancholy degree, to the injury of the wretched individuals themselves, and to that of the community of which it be, comparatively speaking, happy if it could be said they were merely useless members.

In a work of this nature we conceive that we may with peculiar propriety address ourselves to gentlemen of your profession for countenance and assistance, which we earnestly solicit as a powerful means of advancing the important ends proposed—of leading from ignorance and error to piety and virtue, the immediate objects of our protection, and by this happy change to render an essential service to religion and to our country.

By order of the Committee.

HENRY THORNTON, Chairman.

Accompanying all the circulars issued by the Society about this time, there was a set of printed suggestions to the number of ten, intended to aid those who were disposed to engage in the work, but were inexperienced. They were addressed to the "Masters and Mistresses of Sunday Schools."

They were enjoined to inform themselves as to the best method of instruction, and strictly to practice it, and to see that the children read well, and that they understand what they read. Neither writing nor arithmetic was to be taught on the Sabbath.

It was suggested that they require nothing of the children but what they could and should do, but to be sure that all that was required was done. Our modern Sabbath Schools are very deficient in this—we give out lessons, and find the children on the next Sabbath in their places, it is true, but without having looked at their lessons. The only remedy for this is for teachers to study their lessons so thoroughly as to impart interest to the children. They were to keep account of the attendance, and when any were absent to look after them—they were to keep the visiters advised of the improvement and behavior of their scholars, and to arrange them in classes according to their several abilities.

Corporeal punishment was then deemed necessary even in Sabbath Schools—but teachers were advised to use every other means first. Thanks to these suggestions, it was soon found that such punishment was entirely unnecessary.

The crowning thought to be impressed upon the youthful mind, was the *religious* object of the Society; they were to be warned against the evil effects of sin in general, and of particular sins—such as pride, theft, idleness, lying, profanity, disobedience to parents, &c. The precepts of the Bible in regard to these sins were to be explained to them, with the consequences of obedience or disobedience, in such language as they could understand, with such other instruction as the various teachers were capable of giving.

CHAPTER VI.

THE good effect of distributing the plans of the Society, with their accompanying circulars may be seen by the following correspondence. It not only placed many friends of the cause in communication with the society but induced good men to interchange views with each other on the subject, the result of which was always beneficial.

In a letter written by the poet, William Cowper, to the Rev. John Newton of London, and dated Olney, Sept. 24, 1785, he says:

DEAR SIR—Mr. Scott, (Rev. Thomas Scott, author of Scott's Notes on the Bible,) called upon me yesterday; he is much inclined to set up a Sunday School if he can raise a fund for that purpose. Mr. Jones has had one some time at Clifton, and Mr. Unwin, Rector of Stock in Essex, writes me word that he has been thinking of nothing else, day and night, for a fortnight. It is a wholesome measure, that seems to bid fair to be pretty generally adopted, and for the good effects that it promises deserves well to be so.

I know not, indeed, while the spread of the gospel continues so limited as it is how a reformation of manners in the lower class of mankind, can be brought to pass, or by what other means the utter abolition of all principle among them, moral as well as religious, can be prevented. Heathenish parents can only bring up heathenish children, an assertion nowhere oftener or more clearly illustrated than at Olney; where children of seven years of age, infest the streets every evening with curses and songs, to which it would be unseemly to give their proper epithet.

Such urchins as these could not be so diabolically accomplished, unless by the connivance of their parents; it is well, indeed, if, in some instances, their parents are not their instructors. Judging by their proficiency, one can hardly suppose any other. It is therefore doubtless, an act of the greatest charity to snatch the mout of such hands before the inveteracy of the evil shall have made it desperate.

Rev. Daniel Turner, a Baptist minister, and personal friend of Mr. Fox, writes to that gentleman from Abingdon, December 24, 1785; this letter not only approves of the Sunday Schools, but shows the caution necessary to introduce other books than those few with which the society set out. He says:

Dear Sir—I am much obliged to you for your favor of the 16th by Brother ———. I directed and sent the other little packets, as desired, to the clergy of our town.

The importance of the subject referred to in your letter is certainly very great; and I rejoice to find gentlemen of such consequence, as I see in your enclosed representations of the case in London, have espoused the cause of religion and virtue with so much wisdom and zeal. We have begun a plan of the same nature here which is carrying into execution; and I hope upon a more liberal principle than was at first apprehended. A handsome subscription is raised for the purpose.

Your plan is excellent, and I trust will be a guide and pattern for our people.

There is too much of the spirit of bigotry amongst the church party here, but the more sensible begin to be ashamed of it, and I hope we shall be able to do something for the purpose, without any extra assistance. The only defect I see in your plan, (at present,) is your confining the children's reading and attention to the spelling book, Bible and Testament. In some places they take in Dr. Watt's first and second sets of catechisms, especially the first and his little songs for children, even where the church catechism is taught; catechising is a very useful part of the Lord's day exercise, and there is nothing of party there. His first set of catechisms are so peculiarily adapted to open the young mind and gain its attention, that I look upon them, (as many of the establishment do,) of great consequence in the business of religious instruction. And his divine and moral songs, children will early learn and understand, which will render their business pleasing and delightful, as I have found by long experience.

The ignorance of our poor is astonishing, considering they are born in a Christian and Protestant country. Last summmer as I went to visit a friend who lives at a little village in the country belonging to our parish; a poor girl about eight or nine years old, in appearance one of the villagers, accosted me with,

"Pray, Sir, for God's sake, give me a half-penny."

I asked her who or what God was, for whose sake she asked for the half-penny.

"I don't know, Sir," was her answer.

"Who made you?" said I.

"I was not made, Sir, I was born," said the girl, which showed me she was no fool.

"Don't you see the sun there, that shines upon you?" said I.

"Yes, Sir."

"Who made that sun, or put it there, do you think?"

"I don't know, Sir."

"What! did your mother never tell you anything about God?"

"No, Sir."

'Did you never go to church?"

"Yes, Sir."

"Did you not hear something about God at church?"

"No, Sir, [not] as I know of."

I gave her something with some instructions about God, and that she should mind what she heard when she went to church, &c., and left her, lamenting the ignorance of these poor creatures, vast numbers of whom we have everywhere about us.

Many in this town, and in the streets where I dwell, who never, or very seldom, go to any place of public worship, and cannot read, or if they do now and then attend, yet for the want of previous knowledge of the leading principles of religion, they don't understand scarcely anything they hear in the prayers or sermons. And yet there is hope that many of these unhappy creatures may be brought to know something that concerns their present duty towards God and man, and their future happiness by means of these Sunday Schools, who otherwise would live and die in gross ignorance. And I have the more hope of this because there appears amongst many of them, an earnest desire of being instructed. I have had several apply to me to be put to school, and not only parents for their children, but children grown up for themselves, some of whom could not read. It was out of my power to answer all their requests as I wished, and this has been the case with respect to several of my friends who were disposed to send their children to school. This last summer I gave public notice on Lord's-day in our place of worship, that I would catechise the children of our congregation, whose parents were willing to send them, and instead of ten or a dozen of our own people's children, I had nearly fifty of poor, ignorant, ragged wretches, that begged to be instructed. I could not deny them. Some of them could not read, but they would learn the catechism by hearing it read by others. I found no small fatigue in the business, but the pleasure I had in seeing so many poor, ignorant creatures eager to receive instruction, and profit by it in the knowledge of God and religion amply rewarded me, so that I never engaged in any service that gave me more inward satisfaction and delight. The catechisms I taught and endeavored to explain to them, were Dr. Watts' first and second sets, as their capacity and age rendered more suitable.

To these I added also the Doctor's divine songs for children, with which they were highly delighted, as well as instructed. From these circumstances I gather hopes that Sunday Schools here will be useful.

I suppose among the children who may attend the

established worship, the church catechism only, will be taught, but amongst those who attend our places of worship we shall use Dr. Watts' with his divine songs. I wish the narrow spirit of bigotry may give way amongst those of the establishment, to use that catechism with our own and with his divine songs. There is nothing of party or of the difference between the church and dissenters there, and nothing of the kind so well adapted for beginners in the school of Christian knowledge, the ideas and language are so easy, even to a child.

Mr. Turner, in a postscript to this letter, suggests that as the Society had not adopted any catechism, it would be well for them to take that of Dr. Watts with his divine songs; I do not find that his hints were acted upon.

Mr. Fox received a letter about the same time from a lawyer, Mr. J. Huntingford, a warm friend of the Society. The anecdote he tells of himself shows that the disciples of Blackstone were held in the same estimation then that some of them are now. Whether justly or not, I do not pretend to say. His letter is dated Odiham, December 24, 1785. He says—

Sir—Excuse me in recommending that a plan, &c., be sent to the Rev. Dr. Decker, of Halyborn, near Alton, who has ever been zealous in promoting the end of your institution, and in whom I make no doubt you will find a warm advocate. He is the curate of Alton, where he will be assisted by persons different to some whom I meet with here.

On receiving yours, I addressed a letter to the officers of this parish, pointing out the intention and utility of your Society, this letter I entrusted to the care of the most sensible and judicious man among them, (a friend of the plan,) who waited on the vicar with it, and begged his countenance. You remember my telling you the treatment which I formerly met with in proposing a scheme of education somewhat of a similar nature. The first reply from our vicar was, "that attornies were improper persons to have any concern in parochial business, and as to the plan, however proper it may be, yet being proposed by me, he was certain it would not be adopted!"

He added, "but if the parish would agree to clothe and educate a few children, so as to take in those of his groom, he would agree to it without any assistance from your society."

May I trouble you to inform me whether you expect any, and what proportion of the expenses, to be stipulated for, and whether the allowing clothing of any sort is not foreign to your design?

I cannot conclude without expresing my thanks to you for the genteel manner in which you communicated the honor done me by the Society. To them please to present my respectful acknowledgments, and request their permission that my name may be enrolled among the guinea subscribers, and assure them that I am on all occasions, theirs, &c.

Mr. Fox had written a friendly letter to an old acquaintance near Bourton-on-the-water, William Wilkins, Esq., informing him of the aims and objects of the Society, and soliciting his co-operation. The reply of Mr. Wilkins presents a very dark picture of the moral and intellectnal condition of the people around him, and as it varies from any other in some important particulars, I will give it entire. It was addressed to Mr. Fox from—

LITTLE RISINGTON, Dec. 29, 1785.

DEAR SIR—It is not my indifference or indolence that prevents my making a better report to you of the Sunday School scheme in this neighborhood; there are few resident clergy, and few others to be found in the different parishes around us, I may say scarcely any who will patronize, encourage, countenance, or enforce the plan, there are few parishes that can furnish a person competent to the task of teaching, such is the state of the lowest class, and without compulsion they would have very few scholars who could and would teach. What can a single individual do in such a complication of obstacles? Sigh and pray he may and does, but that faith which shall remove mountains, who can find?

Your printed letter, &c., which I have circulated among the most respectable clergy, &c., around this neighborhood, affords me a fresh and good opportunity to make an attempt at an humble imitation of your society. I shall try to bring them, if possible, to make Stow the centre of a society which shall hold forth encouragement to all the neighboring villages to promote religious knowledge, and a reformation of manners among them.

No other scheme seems feasible to me for various reasons. Such a society, if respectable, would have influence, ability, and weight; parish officers, without whom nothing can be done for the purpose around us, would be influenced to exert themselves, the clergy and the gentry would feel themselves engaged to countenance in this case, and without some such plan there is languor, listlessness, &c., to say the least of it, which will defeat and murder the intention.

Should the plan take place, you will probably hear of it, and till the issue of my attempts to accomplish it be known, I do not think it worth while to trouble your society with any application for assistance in any particular village, though I could well dispense it in this place where I live, under my own inspection if afforded. The circulation of your plans, &c., through the kingdom, is, I think, an excellent effect of your institution, in itself considered, and that especially as it holds forth to the whole world, a specimen of liberality of mind of the present race of church men and dissenters, and may be a means of disseminating and perpetuating this desirable and amiable spirit far and wide, to allow each other to think and judge for ourselves and to agree to act together, so far as practicable for the glory of God, and the good of mankind, is the spirit and glory of true Christianity, and I envy the happiness of that man who has realized a wish or a thought to promote it.

I must confess I have no clear ideas after all, of what your society will be willing to do for any particular place, or how they mean to do it, or whether assistance is to be asked upon a formed plan, or direction and assistance sought for together, if there be any such rule limiting the number of books to be given, &c., if they mean entirely or only partially to support a school in any given place, leaving the terms to the parties applying, &c., but I will not tease you with more of my impertinences, as I doubt not the mail coaches will be charged with them as plentifully as they are with hares and partridges at this season of the year.

With warmest respect, I remain,

Dear sir, yours,

W. Wilkins.

CHAPTER VII.

The first report of the Society was made January 11, 1786. The following extract from that report will give an idea of the progress made in the first four months of its existence.

"Your Committee have established five schools in the vicinity of London, and have, in reply to many applications which have been made to them from various parts of the country, signified their disposition to assist in the establishment of schools in those places upon the principles laid down by the Society.*

"Other applications are under their consideration—and from the information already received, they are persuaded the beneficial influence of the Society is becoming more extensive. In order to guard against any possible inconvenience that may arise from boys

* It does not appear from any of the papers of the Society in my hands what those principles were. It is probable that the Society helped any given enterprise as much as they helped themselves. P.

and girls being together in the same schools, your Committee have thought it expedient to the resolution, that in all schools supported by this Society, the boys and girls should be separately instructed—the boys by men and the girls by women—the Committee reserving to themselves any exception to this resolution which may, upon representation, appear necessary."

The subscription already received for the support of the Society, amounted to £987 0s. 6d., (nearly five thousand dollars)—certainly a very creditable beginning, equal to fifteen thousand dollars per annum.

The following very encouraging letters from the Bishops of Salisbury and Landaff to the Chairman of the Executive Committee, were read at this meeting by Samuel Hoare, Esq., of the Society of Friends.

MENGSWELL HOUSE, Dec. 22, 1785.

Sir—The post has just conveyed to me your letter with its enclosures. A friend from their commencement to Sunday Schools, I have established them in every parish where my property lies, and warmly recommended them in my diocese. I have drawn up regulations for their management, and had a spelling book compiled under my direction for their use. From the experience I have already had of the benefits arising from these institutions to good order, morals and religion, among the lower orders of the people, I feel the most earnest satisfaction at the prospect of their becoming general.

I am, sir, with much regard,

Yours, &c.

S. Sarum.

To Henry Thornton, Esq.

Cambridge, Dec. 20, 1785.

Sir—Allow me to return thanks to the Committee appointed by the Society for the establishment of Sunday Schools, for the communication of their plan. I have long thought favorably of the institution of Sunday Schools, and that experience alone would be the sure test of their utility—yet I have ventured to take some steps towards introducing them into the large towns of my diocese. I pray God to prosper the undertaking which you have so benevolently set on foot.

I am, sir, &c.,

R. Landaff.

To Henry Thornton, Esq.

The Rev. Dr. Kaye, Dean of Lincoln, took a decided stand in favor of Sunday Schools from their commencement—having taken occasion, in delivering a charge to his clergy, to recommend the establishment of Sunday Schools in their several parishes, the Executive Committee solicited the privilege of publishing with their circulars that part relating to Sunday Schools. The Dean complied with their wishes—and after having published it in that manner they were desirous of giving it a more general circulation; therefore Mr. Fox returned thanks for past favors, and solicited further privileges in the following letter, dated

LONDON, February 13, 1786.

Rev. Sir—It is with much pleasure I convey to you the unanimous thanks of the Committee, as well as my own, for your ready compliance with their request to publish the extracts from your excellent charge. Nothing could have gratified them more, or rendered our common cause more essential service. We intend to circulate copies, [a few of which I enclose,] with our plans, not presuming to introduce it into the public papers without your consent first obtained, and which I now solicit as a further means of promoting our design.

It gives us great pleasure to hear of the success of your schools at Lincoln, &c.—nor do I doubt it will afford you equal pleasure to hear of ours. About twenty schools, consisting of thirty children on the average, are established and establishing, and we expect to take on a great many more, besides furnishing books, &c. to a number of places where the poverty of the inhabitants renders it necessary.

That your health may be restored, and your life

spared to witness through a succession of many happy years, the growing advantages arising from Sunday Schools, is the sincere wish of, Rev. Sir,

Yours, &c.,

W. Fox.

The Dean's reply was dated

LINCOLN, February 19, 1786.

Sir—I feel very sensibly the candor with which my plain but earnest endeavors to promote *our* cause have been received and honored by the Committee, and I must relinquish any diffidence of my own, when they think my sentiments may be in the least degree instrumental in promoting this great work beyond the limits my own immediate charges, my parish and archdeaconry. For in Lincoln I consider myself as only acting in common with a most respectable and benevolent set of men.

The Committee will therefore be pleased to dispose of the extract in any manner they may think proper.

On seeing it in print some verbal repetitions have struck me, which I had not observed before; however I have let them remain, and have only marked the errata which were possibly in the manuscript.

When I had last the pleasure of seeing you, I mentioned that a committee of correspondence might be very beneficial to the object we had in view—which met with your approbation, and you seemed to wish me to take some conduct of it; but having resigned my subalmoner's office, my preferment is wholly in the country. The former kept me at times nearly half the year in town—the latter, in its different kinds, though adjoining to each other, will admit of but little absence from the whole.

I mentioned this measure also to our friend Mr. Hanway, both at his own house and that of the Marine Society—but his attention was at that time so occupied by some extension of that excellent institution, which peculiarly indeed claimed a preference in his thoughts, that he did not see the necessity of it in the light it appeared to me. I hoped by such establishment that we should give information of the various regulations which had been adopted, and have known how far each had succeeded in experience, or been defective, and it would have been a centre of general support.

I can speak feelingly to this point, for I am persuaded that we should have established our schools here much earlier if I had had more previous communications—and I should certainly have established them in my own parish sooner but for this cause. There are some points yet on which I could wish to be more informed, from the experience of earlier establishments, though the discretion of those I am acting with here has supplied much want of information.

But the respectable Society now formed in London will reach all these wants and gratify our joint wishes —and they may depend upon every circumstantial communication from Lincoln and from Nottinghamshire. I can assure you not a month has passed without suggesting some article of improvement; and in visiting the schools to-day for an absent governor, I observed occurrences of some moment, at the same time we simplify our regulations as much as possible, an object never to be lost sight of where numbers are concerned.

I am, sir, with sincere regard,

Yours, &c.,

R. KAYE.

To Wm. Fox, Cheapside.

Dr. Kaye having given his consent to the more general publication of the extracts from his charge, extends his letter, making suggestions with regard to a committee of correspondence, which Mr. Fox fully approved and afterwards adopted.

The Mariners' Society he speaks of in connection with Mr. Hanway, was founded by that gentleman for the benefit of seamen.

The following are the extracts from the charge of the Dean to his clergy.

" The last time we met I expressed my wishes that such persons as were discharged from the naval and military service on conclusion of the war, might be domesticated and employed as soon as possible in their respective parishes, and that we might endeavor by the kind offices of society, and by general example, to make them become good citizens in time of peace.

" And it does not appear, from the catalogue of those who have lately suffered capital punishment, that these men have been marked in the great delinquency of the times—but a more melancholy inference must be drawn from this circumstance, that the late increase of capital crimes does not proceed from the close of the war, an event to which it might with some plausibility have been attributed, but from the universal depravity of the people—the contemplation of which would be a gloomy office indeed, if it did not appear that in the midst of judgment God had remembered mercy.

" And the divine goodness seems to have pointed out to the present age a measure so peculiarly comprehensive in the advantages which it holds out to society, that it appears formed to counteract every evil propensity of these days, and to prevent them from being injurious to succeeding generations,—which fold, my brethren, within its benevolent arms, every sect of Christianity, every description of mankind.

" The measure which appears to me to possess this

invaluable antidote to the poisonous manners of this depraved age, is the establishment of Sunday Schools. The power and efficacy of these institutions reach to such extent of situation and of numbers, as no other mode of improvement can possibly equal. Having anxiously watched their infancy, and attended to their progress, I have thought their principles the most unequivocal, and their influence the most extensive that can be employed in the cause of general reformation.

The due observance of the Sabbath is the first point inculcated by these institutions, and the mind is formed in its earliest apprehension, thus to feel the just value of this great security of its future conduct; for among the chief causes which the unhappy victims to the laws of their country allege for their ruin, the breach of the Sabbath must ever be accounted the first step in guilt, as it takes place before they are capable of the crimes of more mature age.

"The habit of subordination is by no means a circumstance of trivial moment, as it qualifies such children for the future relations of the community, and the cleanliness which is required in all contributes to their health, and impresses them with a sense of decency.

"These essential articles must meet with universal approbation even from those few who yet object to the further instruction of the lower ranks of life; but this opinion is now reduced to so narrow a ground as scarcely to meet our attention—and I will add that instruction in reading forms a considerable part of these excellent institutions.

"Nor will the benefit be solely confined to the children who partake of these benevolent aids—it will importantly affect the manners of the families, and even of the neighborhood to which they belong.

"In the larger towns the obligation of these establishments is more strongly marked—and the capital of this country has given a most laudable example, by the early adoption of them; but I am persuaded that there are few parishes where there will not be found children to be benefitted by these institutions, whose parents cannot be prevailed upon, perhaps can scarcely be expected, at least in a political view, to spare them for instruction on the days of labor.

"And in manufacturing establishments, they who profit by the labor of such poor children will, we trust, universally recompense them with the humane return. Most benevolent examples have already been given, and I am confident that all the proprietors of such manufactories will, on reflection, consider it as a most solemn and responsible duty, since the children they employ on the days of labor are thereby deprived of the advantage of every other improvement.

"This object, my reverend brethren, I own to you, is nearest my heart in my present communication with you—it is a measure so unequivocal in its principles, so universal in its extent, so providentially pointed out to correct the degeneracy of the present times, that you cannot employ your influence in more humanity to individuals, and more patriotism to your country, than by giving it every assistance and protection in your power."

The following letter from Mr. Fox to Dr. Kaye, the Dean of Lincoln, is important if for no other reason than that it is the first suggestion in favor of auxiliary societies, and is another evidence of the right man in the right place. His mind seemed to keep in advance of all others with regard to the importance of organized and systematic action. The letter was probably written in March.

LONDON, [date not given.]

Rev. Sir—Had the conversation and interview to which you allude in a letter of the 19th of February, left no impression on my mind, the recent favors I have received from you demand my warmest gratitude. Be assured, sir, as nothing lies so near my heart as that cause in which we are mutually embarked, so nothing can afford me equal pleasure to that of hearing from, or communicating to others, an account of its success. Fully convinced that such kind of intercourse would correct some errors, and furnish many useful hints, I mentioned in the very infancy of the Society, that it was your opinion as well as mine, a committee of correspondence should be appointed. This however being mentioned only as an opinion, and the immediate necessity of adopting it not then appearing, the business was postponed till a resolution to circulate our plan and your extract, (a few copies of which, with the amendments, are now enclosed,) through the different counties of England rendered it necessary. From this general circulation, however, it is intended to except all those places where Sunday Schools are already established—and this leads me to request of you, sir, to state their progress in your neighborhood.

"The circulation of the plan has had, and I trust will still have, its use in stirring up the different towns where it is sent to establish schools, even where the Society can afford them no assistance—and were the clergy to come generally into the measure, as I trust from the pious and laudable example you have set them in your county, they will.

"And were the arguments you have brought forward to be urged by them in favor of the charity, Sunday Schools must become general—and from the institution, thus extended, what have we not to hope.

"While the hand of justice only lops off a few pernicious branches, the measure now adopted, with the blessing of God upon it, will pluck up the evil by the roots. No means then should be left untried that may have a tendency to promote an institution, the object of which is the glory of God, and the good of this as well as future generations.

"Would it not be right, sir, to endeavor to excite larger towns to form themselves into societies, that should hold out encouragement to the neighboring villages? Such societies, if respectable, would greatly promote the reformation we so ardently wish. Nor should we, I trust, refuse to hand out any little aid such laudable exertions might require.

"The enclosed report will inform you of our progress. Since then, however, several more schools have been established, and others assisted with books. Be assured, sir, I am a total stranger to the means by which your extract got into the London papers, as stated in your favor of the 24th of February, and am very sorry to hear it was inserted in so imperfect a manner.

I am, &c.,

WILLIAM FOX.

The report alluded to by Mr. Fox was doubtless the first report of the Society, made Jan. 11, 1786.

At the time of which we write the Bishop of Chester was the Rev. Dr. Porteus, afterwards Bishop of London, whose biographer states that "He had early conceived a very favorable opinion of the plan, and in several instances he privately encouraged it. But as an act of prudence he determined not to give it the sanction of his public approbation till accurate inquiry had enabled him to form a more decided judgment of its real value and its probable effects. When, however, repeated information from various quarters, and particularly from some of the largest manufacturing towns in his diocese, had convinced him that these institutions, wherever the experiment had been fairly tried, had produced, and could not fail to produce, if discreetly regulated, essential benefit, he no longer hesitated in promoting them generally throughout his diocese. With this view, as the wisest and most effectual mode of giving publicity to his sentiments, he addressed to his clergy a very excellent letter, containing in a short compass a plain, temperate and judicious exposition of the advantages of Sunday Schools, and of the rules by which they should be conducted."

CHAPTER VIII.

The following note was sent to Mr. Fox, by order of the Executive Committee at a meeting held in March, 1786, he not being present—

MARCH 22, 1786.

SIR—At a meeting of the Executive Committee, it was Resolved, That the Vice-President and Treasurer, with Mr. Alderman Sanderson, Samuel Thornton, Esq., Thomas Raikes, Esq., and William Fox, Esq.; five members of the Committee be desired to wait on the Archbishops, Bishops, or some of the dignitaries of the Church of England to request one of them to preach a sermon in favor of this Institution, and that the several gentlemen be informed of the resolution, and requested to expedite the business as soon as possible.

WM. JACOBSON, Sec'y.

To WM. FOX, Esq.

At the second quarterly meeting of the Society, held April 12, 1786, the Executive Committee reported that there were two hundred and eighty-five subscribers, whom their second and third rule constituted governors by paying each ten guineas, and that there had been received from them one thousand two hundred and thirteen pounds. That they had purchased one thousand pounds in the four per cent consols, that thirty schools had been established by the Society, containing one thousand one hundred and ten pupils, that they had assisted six schools in the country containing six hundred and eighty scholars. And that including the first quarterly report, (Jan. 11, 1786,) the Society had assisted thirty-six schools containing one thousand seven hundred and ninety pupils.

The committee report having appointed inspectors, whose duty it was to visit the schools and suggest any improvement they might think proper. They express the most lively satisfaction with the general appearance of the schools.

A report was also made at this meeting by the deputation appointed to wait on the Archbishops, Bishops, &c.

They said they had been politely received by the Archbishop of Canterbury, who seemed favorably disposed and agreed to recommend them to his Clergy at his next visitation.

The Bishop of Salisbury, from whom the chairman

of the committee, Mr. Thornton, had received a very encouraging note in December previous, was with the Archbishop at the time, and repeated his assurances of co-operation, and added that he daily experienced the good effect of the schools upon the children, and in some instances on the parents also. It was at this meeting that measures were taken to give a large circulation to the extracts from the Dean of Lincoln's charge to his clergy which you have read in the former chapter.

In the distribution of circulars, Mr. Fox would frequently accompany them with a friendly letter soliciting the co-operation of the person to whom it was addressed. Having in this way corresponded with the Rev. Dr. Evans, of the Baptist Academy at Bristol, Mr. Evans replied under date of May 27, 1786, introducing his friends, Revs. Easterbrook and Brown of the Episcopal Church, to whom Mr. Evans had distributed some of the circulars, and recommending the Society to aid them in any undertaking in which they wished to embark. They had schools already in Bristol, but their success was retarded for want of something to occupy the minds of the children through the week, having neither work nor schools to attend. He spoke, however, of two schools at Mangotsford near Bristol, as being quite flourishing. Mr. Evans tendered his services to the Society in any way he could be useful.

It was not long until Rev. Mr. Easterbrook addressed a letter to Mr. Fox. This letter manifests such a humble, self-sacrificing spirit, and deals so faithfully with the unfaithfulness of professing Christians, that its perusal must be attended with good results. I therefore introduce it in this place. It is dated—

BRISTOL, July 5, 1786.

MY DEAR SIR—Deeply impressed as I am with a grateful sense of the honor you have paid my recommendation of the three poor parishes of Portishead, Weston, and Walton, for the aid of the London Sunday School Society, permit me to return my warmest acknowledgments, for your condescending acquiescence in my request, as well as for the obliging letter which conveyed the satisfactory intelligence.

Indeed the discovery I was obliged to make of the spirit by which you are inflnenced, filled me with gladness and joy, and impressed my mind with much thankfulness to the Donor of every good and perfect gift, for having vouchsafed to bestow upon you such a tender concern for the kingdom and interest of our dear Lord. It is truly lamentable to observe that the genuine friends of our adorable Redeemer are very thinly scattered, even amongst the multitude of professed adherents to his religion. How few are to be found who give proof that they *love our Lord in sincerity.*

How few will abandon their own earthly concerns and *count all things but loss,* if, by any means, they may promote the salvation of sinners, and the glory of Christ! How few pass the time of their sojourning here *looking not at the things which are seen,* but at the things which are not seen? Well, we bless God that one here and there is to be met with of this description, and let us make it matter of daily supplication that he will be graciously pleased to add to their number. Glory be to his name for the effusion of his spirit which he hath poured upon you! I trust that your zeal will provoke many, and that by the united efforts of the people of God in the metropolis, we shall be favored to hear of a cloud of miserable transgressors convinced of their dangerous situation, and brought to fly to Jesus the appointed city of refuge.

I have communicated the account of your Christian assistance, to the Rev. Mr. Brown, who, by this time I take it for granted, hath answered for himself. Wishing you all temporal and eternal blessings,

I am, dear Sir,

Your grateful, &c.,

JOSEPH EASTERBROOK.

To WM. FOX, ESQ.

At the quarterly meeting of the Society for October,

1786, it was reported by the Executive Committee, that they had sent a circular letter to the managers of the schools under the patronage of the Society, requesting that registers might be kept of the names and numbers of the attendants of each school, to be reported to the Society in their quarterly returns; they hoped by this means to secure a more regular attendance on the part of the pupils, and be enabled to determine with greater accuracy the increase or diminution of each school. At this meeting the committee reported the first legacy to the Society. Five hundred pounds having been bequeathed to it by William Denne, Esq., deceased.

Mr. Fox and Mr. Raikes were both indefatigable in their efforts for the advancement of the cause in which they were engaged. The labors of Mr. Fox being connected at all times with the other members of the Executive Committee, together with his native modesty prevent his name from appearing so conspicuous as it otherwise would. On the other hand, Mr. Raikes, equally unassuming, but residing at a distance from the head-quarters of the Society, found it more convenient to co-operate with them by writing, than by being personally present; hence the following letter describing the means taken to divert the minds of the people from the manner in which they had usually spent the Sabbath nearest Michaelmas Day, (September 29,) a Roman Catholic festival that had been observed in the parish of Painswick for many years. Mr. Fox attended the meeting described in this letter, which was directed to the committee of the "Society established in London for the support and encouragement of Sunday Schools in the different counties of England."

GLOUCESTER, Oct. 7, 1786.

Gentlemen—The parish of Painswick exhibited on Sunday, the 24th ult. a specimen of the reform which the establishment of Sunday Schools is likely to introduce.

An annual festival has from time immemorial been held on that day—a festival that would have disgraced the most heathenish nations. Drunkenness and every species of clamor, riot and disorder, formerly filled the town upon this occasion. Mr. Webb, a gentleman who has exerted the utmost assiduity in the conduct of the Sunday Schools in Painswick, was lamenting to me the sad effects that might be naturally expected to arise from this feast. It appeared to us that an attempt to divert the attention of the vulgar from their former brutal prostitution of the Lord's day, by exhibiting to their view a striking picture of the superior enjoyment to be derived from quietness, good order, and the exercise of that benevolence which Christianity peculiarly recommends, was an experiment worth hazarding.

We thought it could do no mischief—it would not

increase the evil. I was immediately determined to invite the gentlemen and people of the adjacent parishes to view the children of the Sunday Schools—to mark their improvement in cleanliness and behaviour, and to observe the practicability of reducing to a quiet and peaceable demeanor the neglected part of the community, those who form the great bulk of the people.

In the parish of Painswick are several gentlemen who have a taste for music, and who immediately offered to give every assistance in a church service; and my benevolent friend, the Rev. Dr. Glasse, complied with our entreaty to favor us with a sermon. Mr. Campbell, a very active Justice of the Peace, Mr. Townsend, Mr. Sheppard, Mr. Webb of Epworth, and several other gentlemen engaged to give their countenance. We were highly gratified too with Mr. Boddington's company, who kindly came from Cheltenham to take a view of this progress in civilization. He is one of your Vice-Presidents, and from his report you will receive a far more perfect idea than my pen can give.

On the Sunday afternoon the town was filled with the usual crowds who attend the feasts, but instead of repairing to the alehouses, as heretofore, they all hastened to the church, which was filled in such a manner as I never remember to have seen any church in this country before. The galleries and the aisles were filled like a playhouse.

Drawn up in rank around the church-yard appeared the children belonging to the different schools, to the number of three hundred and thirty-one. The gentlemen walked round to view them. It was a sight interesting and truly affecting. Young people, lately more neglected than the cattle in the field—ignorant, profane, filthy, clamorous, impatient of every restraint—were here seen cleanly, quiet, observant of order, submissive, courteous in behaviour, and in conversation free from that vileness which marks our wretched vulgar. The inhabitants of the town bear testimony to this change in their manners. The appearance of decency might be assumed for a day, but the people among whom they live are ready to declare that this is a character fairly started.

After the public service, a collection for the benefit of the institution was made at the doors of the church. When I consider that the bulk of the congregation were persons of middling rank, husbandmen and other inhabitants of the adjacent villages, I concluded that the collection, if it amounted to twenty-four or twenty-five pounds, might be deemed a good one.

My astonishment was great indeed when I found that the sum was not less than fifty-seven pounds! This may be accounted for from the security which the establishment of Sunday Schools has given to the property of every individual in the neighborhood. The farmers, &c. declare that they and their families can now leave their homes, gardens, &c., and frequent the public worship without danger of depredation;—formerly they were under the necessity of leaving their servants, or staying at home themselves as a guard; and this was insufficient—the most vigilant were sometimes plundered.

It is not then to be wondered at that a spirit of liberality was excited on this occasion. A carpenter put a guinea in the plate, and afterwards brought four more to Mr. Webb. "It was my fixed design," says he, "to devote the sum that I received for a certain job of work to the support of Sunday Schools. I received five guineas—one only I put in the plate—it did not become me to put more—it would have looked like ostentation; but here are the other four,"—giving them to Mr. Webb. Another instance of spirit occurred in a man upwards of eighty years of age, who seemed about the rank of the yeomanry. "Oh that I should live," said he, "to see this day, when poor children are thus befriended, and taught the road to peace and comfort here, and happiness and heaven hereafter." The old man gave a guinea, and said he would leave another in the hands of a friend, if he should die before the next anniversary. When the matter of the collection was settled, we went to the school to hear what progress was made in reading, &c. The emulation to show their acquirements was so very general, that it would have taken up a day to have gratified all the children.

In the mean time the town was remarkably free from those pastimes which used to disgrace it—wrestling, quarreling, fighting, were totally banished; all was peace and tranquillity.

I fear I have been too prolix, but I could not convey the complete idea that I was desirous of imparting to the governors and promoters of Sunday Schools, without writing these particulars.

I forgot to mention that Wm. Fox, one of the worthy members of your Committee, was present with us at Painswick. The Sunday School was first established at Painswick in the summer of the year 1784. The children had been brought up in total ignorance. Of the number that attend the schools, two hundred and thirty can read in the Bible or Testament, eighty can read in the Sunday Scholar's Companion, and about twenty-one are in the alphabet. These children have no teaching but on the Sunday—what they learn at the leisure hours in the week is the effect of their own desire to improve; many have their books at their looms, to seize any vacant minute when their work is retarded by the breaking of threads.

To relieve the parish from the burden of clothing these poor creatures, Mr. Webb proposed that such children as by increase of industry would bring a penny every Sunday towards their clothing, should be assisted by having that penny doubled. This has had an admirable effect—the children now regularly bring their pence every Sunday. Many of them have been clothed, and the good consequences of laying a little by are powerfully enforced.

It is pretty evident that were every parish in this kingdom blessed with a man or two of Mr. Webb's active turn and benevolent mind, the lower class of people in a few years would exhibit a material change of character, and justify that superior policy which tends to prevent crimes rather than to punish them. The liberality with which the members of your Society have stood forth in this attempt to introduce a degree of civilization and good order amongst the lowest ranks, entitle them to the thanks of the community, and particularly of an individual, who will ever be proud to subscribe himself, &c.

R. Raikes.

P. S.—The gentlemen of Painswick intend making a request to Dr. Glasse to publish his sermon. The happy choice of the text had a remarkable effect in commanding the attention of the audience. The Scriptures could not have furnished a passage more literally applicable to the subject. It was taken from Deut. xxxi. 12, 13—"Gather the people together, men and women, and children, and the stranger that is within thy gates, that they may hear, and that they may learn, and fear the Lord your God, and observe to do all the words of this law, and that their *children which have not known any thing* may hear and learn to fear the Lord your God as long as ye live."

R. R.

CHAPTER IX.

In a former chapter I called the reader's attention to the suggestion by Mr. Fox, that auxiliary societies might be beneficial. It will be seen by the following note that such societies were organized, although not called by that name :

WELDON, June 11, 1787.

DEAR SIR :—I am much obliged by the trouble you took in correcting the plan for our Sunday Schools, and also for procuring the spelling books. I wish you would send me three dozen more the first opportunity. The schools, under the management of the dissenters, far exceed our expectations. We have subscriptions to support fifty-eight scholars. Lord Howard has subscribed four guineas to the dissenters' society, the Mayor of the Corporation, one guinea. The church people have a very large subscription. Although we have separate schools and distinct governments, we are exceedingly friendly, and seem to have one object in view, and that is the good of our fellow-creatures ;

and that it may issue in God's glory, is the ardent wish of

Yours, sincerely,

J. G. Searle.

I have thus far spoken only of those who were friendly to the Sunday-School cause, but as no real benevolent object was ever carried forward without opposition, it would be unreasonable to expect this to be an exception. There are always men of narrow minds and contracted souls, to oppose every good work. They seem to be necessary to stimulate others to the faithful discharge of duty. Indeed, a noble, large-hearted man always appears to better advantage by coming in contact with such selfish, jealous mortals, and as these were found to be quite numerous, both in the established church, and among dissenters, I will give some specimens of their views and Mr. Fox's manner of dealing with them.

Rev. Joseph Ivimey, in his memoir of William Fox, mentions a letter he received from his eldest son, Mr. Jonathan Fox, of Liverpool; this letter, written June 9, 1827, relates entirely to events connected with the organization and early management of the Sunday-School Society. An extract from that letter says :—
"In this endeavor, he was accused by the clergy, and by more than one of its dignitaries, of a design to proselyte and render sectarian the children for whom

he was desirous of obtaining instruction. He was inundated with letters to that effect, and visits were made to him by direction of the hierarchy to ascertain the correctness of that opinion.

"He found, however, ample means to convince them that his only desire was that the poor might be rendered able to read the Holy Scriptures, and therefore, that he had laid it down as a fundamental rule that in all the schools about to be established, the reading lessons should be confined to the Bible. In proof of this, he appealed to the clergymen of the parish of Clapton, as to whether all the objects of his bounty men, women, and children, had not been directed to attend on the Lord's-day at the established church. Indeed, this circumstance had so strongly impressed the mind of that Rev. Divine, when he heard my father was a dissenter, that he earnestly entreated him to attend at church to hear a sermon which he was about to address to the persons who were assisted by him. Upon such an occasion the modesty of my father would not suffer him to attend, fearing he might hear that conduct lauded which he himself had considered as an humble return to the Father of mercies who had made him the almoner of His bounties. The sermon, which was preached to a crowded congregation, it was said was highly interesting and affecting, and very complimentary to my father."

A daughter of Mr. Fox, who survived him, says :—

"I have heard my father say that while the Sunday School Society was in formation, one of the bishops sent his curate to him to learn the nature of the institution, and that the bishop afterwards expressed his entire approbation of the Society, and I think, accompanied it with a donation of £20."

Among dissentors the opposition to Sunday Schools at one time, was quite formidable. George Offor, a magistrate of London, says, in an introduction to an edition of "Bunyan's Pilgrim's Progress," "that not only was that grand work opposed by the friends of Bunyan, both before and after its publication, but that when Sunday Schools first originated, some of the most eminent evangelical dissenting ministers in London, held a conference on the subject of their introduction into that city, when it was pleaded against them, that such schools were the desecration of the Lord's-day, and it was only by a very small majority that they were sanctioned."

Mr. Fox, being a dissenter himself, he felt at liberty not only to explain but to reprove those who were over-anxious lest the dissenting interest should suffer in consequence of the introduction of Sunday Schools by the Society. In answer to a letter from a dissenter in the country expressing his fears, Mr. Fox wrote the following letter some time during the year 1787:

SIR—That a faithful follower of the Redeemer

should refuse to support a cause evidently calculated to promote His glory, and the good of this as well as future ages, because it interferes with his own particular interest, is what I can scarcely persuade myself exists. Animated with love to Christ, and a desire of saving souls, let us not waste a moment in the enquiry, who is of Paul, and who of Apollos? But as the great work of instruction depends under Providence, on the exertions of *every* denomination of Christians, let us make united efforts to save a guilty land from ruin, or at least prevent the evils that now exist from descending to future generations.

And where, sir, can means be found sufficiently extensive, or that promises advantages equally comprehensive, with those held forth in the establishment of Sunday Schools? There at an easy rate, the poor become acquainted with that inestimable book which is able to make them wise unto salvation; and permit me, sir, to say were we sufficiently acquainted with it, and properly affected with the important truths it contains, we should not only pray for a blessing upon it where it is, but should strive by every means in our power to send it where it is not.

Would it be possible, sir, to behold unmoved criminals dying victims to the laws of our country? Or could we revel in luxury while our neighbors were perishing with hunger? And shall we, while in the possession of every spiritual blessing, view with unconcern the multitudes who are perishing around us for lack of knowledge? Forbid the thought. What, has Christ laid down his life for *us*, and shall we refuse a cup of cold water to these little ones.

To teach to read the Bible, inconceivable as the blessing appears, is not the only object of this institution.

Sabbath-breaking, the inlet to all other sins, is hereby prevented, and the children are conducted, clean and decent as circumstances will admit, to places of public worship. And have we not to hope? How many have gone to the house of God through mere necessity, and others from more unworthy motives, when that word they meant to ridicule, sharpened by the Spirit of the Lord, pierced them to the heart. And should one soul be brought to glory by this means, how amply should we be repaid.

He that winneth souls is wise, and they that turn many to righteousness, shall shine as the stars for ever and ever.

After all that has been said, can any of us be so bigoted as to have our minds absorbed in the little distinctions of interest in which we were educated, and judge everything unworthy our notice that does not immediately tend to promote it.

We should do well to consider the ground on which we stand. Are we for Christ? Then we should endeavor to do good to all. But to conclude. If teaching persons to read the Bible, and placing them under the sound of the gospel, (for all the dissenting children, and some of the church, go to meeting,) should injure the dissenting interest, it must be an interest unworthy our support. Give me leave just to add that, in consequence of the plans sent to Colchester, all the ministers, churchmen and dissenters, to the number of sixteen, including a speaker among the Quakers, assembled at the Rev. Dr. Foster's, unanimously agreed to support the institution in that place. Trusting my good friends at ——— will not be outdone in acts of humanity, Christianity, and liberality by any other friends in any other place, and hoping ere long to hear of your success,

I am, &c.,

WM. FOX.

In 1787, Mr. Fox relinquished his business in London to his sons, and removed to a delightful country village called Donnyland, near Colchester, the native place of Mrs. Fox. In his removal to the country, Mr. Fox did not leave his spirit of religion and benevolence behind, but interested himself in behalf of the poor in the vicinity of his new home.

If he did not meet with opposition from the clergyman of the parish, he failed to secure the hearty cooperation of that gentleman in his good work. We have already seen that although Mr. Fox was exceedingly mild and agreeable, he could, when occasion required, administer rebuke in a very pointed manner. The following letter will show that the fact of the delinquent being a minister of the gospel and even of the established church did not deter him. He acted upon the injunction found in Proverbs xxiv. 11, 12. "If thou forbear to deliver them, they are drawn unto death, and those that are ready to be slain. If thou sayest, Behold, we knew it not; doth not he that pondereth the heart, consider it? and he that keepeth thy soul, doth not he know it? and shall he not render to every man according to his works?"

Lord's-day Evening, Jan. 18, 1789.

Rev. Sir—Though it is not more my practice than it is my province to condemn any man, mnch less a clergyman of the Church of England, for "to his own master he standeth or falleth," yet you will permit me, without taking offence, to express my grief at seeing those committed to your care, wander about without a shepherd. The poor, who have little to comfort them besides that which the gospel affords, have at this inclement season, a more than ordinary claim to your labors.

Times of affliction are generally those in which God is more than commonly sought unto. In their affliction they will seek me early. And, indeed, God has said, Call upon me in the day of trouble, I will deliver thee, and thou shalt glorify me. Now, sir, where are those poor, ignorant creatures to look for instruction and assistance in the worship of God, but to their pastor. You have upon you the care of their souls, and they have crowded your church for three succeeding Lord's-days, but with what success, I leave to your determination.

"Have you watched for their souls as one that must give an account. And where is the word so likely to make a divine impression in the heart as when it is softened with affliction. On your candor, and good sense, sir, I rely for the pardon of this intrusion, not doubting that a liberty taken under the impression of love to God, and benevolence to man, will find a ready excuse from a gentleman of your known generosity.

I am, Rev. Sir, respectfully yours,

William Fox.

To the Rev. Mr. Slater.

We have no means of knowing how this faithful rebuke was received, but if Christians would talk thus plainly, and honestly, difficulties would often be checked before growing to such magnitude as to be unmanageable

While engaged with the subject of opposition to Sunday Schools, I will give one more item, although its proper place according to date would be a little further along:

In the Protestant Dissenting Magazine, first volume, published in 1794, there is a letter from one of the country towns some distance from London, stating that Sunday Schools had been in operation there for nine years without giving the least evidence of their having done any good, as no instance of moral improvement had occurred to distinguish Sunday School children from others. The friends of the school having claimed that they would not only have a good effect on the children, but that it would, as in other places, extend to the parents also.

The writer objected to the schools, because he thought the clergy should first teach the parents, and devise means for bettering their condition, that they might be able to educate their own children, we suppose, in the meantime leaving them to grow up in ignorance. He states that he and his friends are very conscientious in their opposition, because they believe it to be a desecration of the Sabbath, and closes with what he supposes an unanswerable argument. He says:—"How can it be expected the Divine Being will sanction the violation of his own laws? or give a blessing to an institution which appears to be contrary to his revealed will?" A writer, quoting from the letter, thinks it should be placed among the curiosities of Sabbath-school literature.

The unhealthy state of the religious mind, as evinced in the above letter, manifested itself in various ways. Sometimes the opposition took quite a ludicrous turn, especially with regard to the schools being a desecration of the Sabbath. This was particularly the case previous to the inauguration of the system of gratuitous teaching. A dignified bishop is mentioned, who proposed to remove the difficulty by holding the *Sunday Schools* on the previous *Saturday afternoon !*

It is pleasant to turn from the timid and halting, and contemplate those who entered heartily into the work, A sketch of a Sunday School enterprise, in which William Wilberforce and Hannah More were the chief actors, will not be found devoid of interest.

William Wilberforce was born in the city of Hull, Yorkshire, England, in 1759 ; he received a thorough education, and very early in life entered the British Parliament, and became a distinguished member. In his younger days, he was remarkable for gaiety and worldliness, and what was equally remarkable, in the height of his successful political career, he became a convert to Christianity, and devoted his talents, wealth, and learning to its advancement. He is the author of many valuable works in favor of the Christian religion. The most distinguished act of his life, was being the chief agent in causing the English government to abolish the slave trade, and finally, to emancipate every slave in her dominions. He died in 1833, and was buried in Westminster Abbey.

Miss Hannah More was distinguished for her literary productions, always in favor of Christianity. Her religion, however, was not all theoretical; she was willing to put it in practice, and go about doing good. At the special request of Mr. Wilberforce, she undertook the task of introducing Sunday Schools into Cheddar, England. In a letter to him, to procure books from the Sunday School Society, for the use of her schools in Cheddar, she describes the opening of her first school by saying:—"It was an affecting sight. Several of the grown-up youths had been tried at the last Assizes; three were the children of a person lately condemned to be hanged—many, thieves! All ignorant, profane, and vicious beyond belief. Of this banditti, we have enlisted one hundred and seventy; and when the clergyman, a hard man, who is also the magistrate, saw these creatures kneeling around us, whom he had seldom seen but to commit, or to punish in some way, he burst into tears. I can do them little good, I fear, but the grace of God can do all. Your friend, Henry Thornton, thought we ought to try."

In a postscript to the same letter, she describes an incident that occurred upon her dismissing the first school. She says:—"Some musical gentlemen, drawn from a distance by curiosity, just as I was coming out of the church with my ragged regiment, much depressed to think how little good I could do them, quite unexpectedly struck up that beautiful and animating anthem, 'Inasmuch as ye did it to one of the least of these, ye have done it unto me.' It was well performed, and had a striking effect."

In a letter to Mr. Wilberforce, in 1791, Miss More gives quite a history of her schools, showing the extreme wretchedness of the poor people in England at that time. It appears that, after reconnoitering until they found what a miserable condition the inhabitants were in, she and her sister went and put up at a public house, perplexed as to the best mode of inaugurating the business. There were over two thousand people in the parish, all very poor except about a dozen wealthy farmers, and they were exceedingly coarse and ignorant. These two ladies visited every house. They say they proceeded like fortune-tellers. From each family they would get the name and character of the next. When informed that they were going to open a school for the poor, the farmers did not like it. They rented a dwelling for themselves, and went at their work as real missionaries. Next to the house they rented was an ox-house or stable ; this they had repaired for a schoolroom. During their visits they saw but one Bible in the place, and that was used to prop a flower-pot.

They induced the mothers to bring their children together on a week-day, and selected their scholars, and took a list of the names. Paid teachers, as we have shown, proved a great drawback to the Sunday Schools—but this, we believe, is the only place where parents refused to send their children unless *they* were paid for it. Others feared to send the children lest the teachers, at the end of seven years, should have such power over them as to send them beyond sea. Another difficulty was to find teachers. They were fortunate in finding two, a mother and daughter. Thus the school was opened. At the end of one year they found they had gained strength with the poor, but persecution from the rich ; having the windows of their schoolroom occasionally broken. Yet much good was done with old and young. Bibles began to be distributed as rewards to the diligent only. An anniversary festival was instituted, at which the journal was read for the year, and a general report of the progress of the schools. At the end of six years the schools in Cheddar had two hundred children and over two hundred elder persons constantly in attendance.

CHAPTER X.

A YOUNG Cornish miner, by the name of Richard Rodda, was converted in early life under the preaching of some of Mr. Wesley's "helpers," and not long after, impressed for the British navy. A good Quaker passing was moved with sympathy at his innocent appearance, and by his kind intervention the boy was rescued from the temptations of a sailor's life. While yet a miner he was accustomed to lay down his tools in the depths of the earth, and indulge in secret prayer.

Dr. Stevens, in his "History of Methodism," relates an incident in which his life was saved by one of these simple acts of devotion. "He had knelt but about two minutes when the earth gave way above him; a large stone fell before him and reached above his head; another fell at his right hand, and a third on his left, each, like the first, being higher than himself; a fourth fell upon these about four inches above him, and sheltered him. Had he been in any other posture than that of his devotions, he would, he says, 'have been crushed to pieces.'"

Not long after this he gave himself up entirely to religious labors, and became a Methodist minister. He would often preach in the open air, the only notice being the announcement of a text or the singing of a hymn. He was often assailed by mobs, pelted with dirt and broken tiles, and on one occasion he was so besmeared with mud that he had to desist for the time. Among such scenes as these he would often draw tears from the eyes of those who came to disturb him. After establishing a reputation as an able and eloquent minister of the gospel and laboring forty-five years, he fell with his face to the enemy.

Such was the man to whom the Rev. John Wesley, in writing a letter from London, June 17, 1787, uses the following language:

"My Dear Brother—I am glad you have taken in hand that blessed work of setting up Sunday Schools in Chester. It seems these will be one great means of reviving religion throughout the nation. I wonder Satan has not sent out some able champion against them."

The schools alluded to by Mr. Wesley had been organized by the Rev. Mr. Rodda in 1786, and at the time he received Mr. Wesley's note he had nearly seven hundred children under regular masters.

That note to Rev. Mr. Rodda was neither the first nor the last attention Mr. Wesley gave to Sabbath Schools. In his private journal, July 18, 1784, he says: "I find these schools spring up wherever I go; perhaps God may have a deeper end therein than men are aware of. Who knows but some of these schools may be nurseries for Christians?"

In January, 1785, Mr. Wesley published all that Mr. Raikes had written on Sunday Schools, in his Arminian Magazine, and recommended them to his people. He says that in 1786 five hundred and fifty children were taught in the Sunday Schools of his Society at Bolton, and the next year he found there eight hundred, taught by eighty masters.

On the eighteenth of April, 1788, Mr. Wesley preached at Wigan "A Sermon for the Sunday Schools," and "the people flocked from all quarters in a manner that never was known before."

In 1790, just the year before his death, Mr. Wesley wrote to the Rev. Charles Atmore, an itinerant preacher, and says—"Dear Charles, I am glad you have set up Sunday Schools at Newcastle. This is one of the best institutions which has been seen in Europe for some centuries."

We will return to Mr. Fox, who, whether he lived in town or country, was ever active in promoting the cause for which the Society was instituted, as may be seen from the ensuing letter to the Executive Committee.

DONNYLAND HALL, in Essex, Jan. 21, 1787.

Gentlemen—If it cannot be said that the parish of East Donnyland exhibits a scene of the greatest poverty, it may be truly said that the inhabitants are abandoned to every species of vice. Situated near the sea, on which the greater part of them are employed, and at about a mile distant from the church, which stands within the parish and near the Hall, every day seems alike—hence arises that depravity of morals and those depredations to which we are perpetually liable.

I have taken some pains to procure a list of the ignorant, and have offered to contribute towards the support of a school, as well as to make application to the Committee for a supply of books. A meeting convened for this purpose was held this day at the church—when to my great surprise there appeared nearly sixty of both sexes, including several parents, who were real objects of charity, and seemed truly solicitous to partake of its benefits. Nor was this the only gratifying spectacle. It was truly affecting to see the old people entreating to be taught to read the Bible. It also gave me great pleasure to receive application from persons in better circumstances, who, in order to countenance the design, and set an example to their poor neighbors, offered to subject their children, though they could read, to the same regulations, and to bear their expense.

Lest I should be thought tedious upon a subject on which I could with pleasure dwell, I shall conclude with making a request that forty spelling books, twenty Testaments, and four Bibles be sent for the use of two schools. It would have given me pleasure could the village have borne the whole expense. Though the rector and parish at large concur in the measure, nothing but the bare instruction can be expected. I am, gentlemen,

Yours respectfully,

W. Fox.

It was concerning the negligence of the rector of the parish towards the children of these schools, that Mr. Fox, two years later, wrote the very pointed letter of rebuke given in the chapter next preceding this.

Colchester, where the sixteen ministers met upon receiving the plans of the Society, and resolved to support Sunday Schools, was not far from Donnyland. In June of this year (1787) the friends of Sunday Schools resolved to hold a public meeting. The following extract of a letter from Mr. Fox to his friend and fellow laborer Mr. Raikes, will give an idea of the exercises on that occasion.

"Not a single occurrence interposed to embitter or in the least interrupt the pleasures of the day. All was harmony, peace and love—for however divided in political sentiments, or separated from each other by diversity of religious opinions, in this important undertaking, wherein the glory of God and the good of mankind are so intimately concerned, the most perfect unanimity has from its commencement prevailed. How worthy of imitation is this example. Should it be universally followed, and should that spirit of bigotry which disgraced former times, and in some instances prevents improvements in the present, be proscribed from the breasts of all, as it is from the wise and good, we might expect to see, not only two hundred and thirty-four thousand poor children which the Sunday Schools in England are now calculated to contain, emerging from ignorance and rescued from vice, but such an extension of the institution as could not fail, under the divine blessing, to produce universal good to the poor, and security to the rich."

To this letter the following reply was sent by Mr. Raikes:

GLOUCESTER, July 12, 1787.

Dear Sir—I regret that the variety of my business and engagements, when I was last in town, prevented me from devoting an afternoon to the enjoyment of your society. The loss was mine—for I find few pleasures equal to those which arise from the conversation of men who are endeavoring to promote the glory of the Creator and the good of their fellow creatures. I consider you, too, with the greater respect, as I believe you were one of my first encouragers at the outset of the little plan I was the humble instrument of suggesting to the world.

I thank you, my good friend, for communicating the pleasing recital from Colchester. What a wide and extensive field of rational enjoyment opens to our view, could we allow the improvement of human nature to become the source of pleasure.

Instead of training horses to the course, and viewing with delight their exertions at New Market, let our men of fortune turn their eyes to an exhibition like that of Colchester. Impart to them a small portion of solid enjoyment, which a mind like yours must receive from the glorious sight. Children more neglected than the beasts of the field, now taught to relish the comfort of decency and good order, and to know that their own happiness greatly depends on promoting the happiness of others.

When the community begins to reap the benefit of these principles, let us hope that this nation will manifest to the world the blessed effects of a general diffusion of Christianity. The great reformers of past times have been only removing obstructions in our way. Let us hope that the day is approaching when "the knowledge of the Lord shall cover the earth as the waters cover the sea." The number of children admitted into a state of culture in this short period, seems to me little less miraculous than the draught of fishes, and would incline us to think that the prophecy above quoted is advancing to its completion.

Some French gentlemen, members of the Royal Academy at Paris, were with me last week, and were so strongly impressed with the probable effects of this scheme of civilization, that they have taken all the pieces I have printed on the subject, and intend proposing establishments of a similar nature in some of their parishes in the provinces, by way of experiment. We have seen the rapid progress of Christianity. Dr. Adam Smith, who has so ably written on the wealth of nations, says—"No plan has promised to effect a change of manners with equal ease and simplicity, since the days of the apostles."

I have sent you my paper of this week that you may see we are extending toward Wales, with the improvement of a school of industry.

I am, dear sir, your sincere friend, &c.,

R. RAIKES.

P. S.—Send me the World, in which the Colchester letter appeared.

Mr. Fox had published his account of the Colchester anniversary in a paper called the "World."

The following extract of a letter from Mr. Fox to the Rev. [afterward] Dr. Duncan, an Independent minister of Winborne, Dorsetshire, will throw more light on a subject that has been alluded to before.

DONNYLAND, July 20, 1787.

Rev. Sir—Though since my retirement to this delightful situation I have been much taken up with its native beauties, I have not forgotten my promise to correct an error in the preface of your excellent little Catechism for the benefit of Sunday Schools. Permit me then to say, sir, in justice to Mr. Raikes, that instead of his early adopting the Sunday Schools established by the London Society, you will find by the enclosed extract that the Society took the hint from him—and it will barely be possible to set forth their utility in stronger language than that used by himself in a letter to a friend."

The remainder of this letter was a quotation from Mr. Raikes, June 5, 1784. describing his conversation with Mr. Church, a manufacturer of hemp and flax.

The Society had been in existence near two years, and although Mr. Raikes was at all times actively engaged in promoting its interests, he was not a member until July 11, 1787. At a general meeting of the Society, the Executive Committee offered the following—

"Your Committee taking into consideration the humble zeal and merits of Robert Raikes, Esq., of Gloucester, who may justly be considered as the original founder as well as a liberal promoter of Sunday Schools, beg leave to recommend to the general meeting that he be chosen as honorary member of this Society."

The report was unanimously adopted—thus Mr. Raikes became the first honorary member of a Sunday School Society.

At a meeting of the Society, Oct. 10, 1787, two years and one month after its organization, it was reported that they had established and assisted two hundred and eighty-two schools, containing upwards of sixteen thousand pupils—that the several schools had been supplied with 20,295 spelling books, 6,217 Testaments, and 1,141 Bibles.

The annual report of the Society for 1788, as signed by the auditors Jan. 17, 1789, shows that at the beginning of the year there was a balance of five hundred and twenty pounds fourteen shillings and one penny, in the hands of the Treasurer. That the donations and annual subscriptions for that year amounted to seven hundred and five pounds, one shilling and three pence. That the total of collections at places of public worship was one hundred and seventy-four pounds one shilling and six pence ; and that for half a year's dividend on fifteen hundred pounds invested in four per cent. annuities, the Society had received sixty pounds ; and that schools assisted by the Society with books, had returned in cash twenty-one pounds and sixteen shillings. Total receipts for the year, one thousand four hundred and eighty-one pounds twelve shillings and ten pence.

The Society paid out in the mean time to teachers in the different schools, two hundred and seventy-six pounds eleven shillings and six pence ; for office rent, seventeen pounds and seventeen shillings ; for printing, stationery, books for the schools, Secretary's pay, and sundry incidentals, seven hundred and sixteen pounds ten shillings and two pence. Total amount of disbursements for the year, one thousand and ten pounds eighteen shillings and eight pence, leaving a balance in the treasury of four hundred and seventy pounds fourteen shillings and two pence.

It will be seen that of the disbursements considerably more than one fourth was paid to teachers.

At this meeting the Society reports the number of schools established and assisted from the organization of the Society, 610. Scholars, 41,295. Spelling books given away, 45,639. Testaments 13,144. Bibles 3,261.

In the year 1790 the following circular was issued

by the Executive Committee and addressed to various persons throughout the country.

LONDON.

Sir—As in the present intercourse among nations, a wider field of inquiry and observation is opened to the man of genius than at any former period, it is not to be wondered at that prejudices imbibed in youth, and which in less enlightened times set mankind at variance when ripened into age, should now subside. Science and liberality of sentiment commonly go hand in hand—but while the principles of equity, moderation and benevolence prevail in a considerable degree among the higher orders of the people, it is much to be lamented that disorders of the most pernicious tendency pervade the lower ranks, and that reformation with respect to them has, till of late, been rather a matter of solicitude and desire, than of serious expectation.

Happily however, not only for the present but also for future generations, a remedy for these evils has been discovered in the establishment of Sunday Schools, of the success of which the Society has received the most indubitable proofs. Embracing the illiterate poor of every description, they promise fair to eradicate in a very great degree those vicious habits, and that consequent wretchedness, which have at all times been so much deplored.

That Sabbath-breaking may be prevented, and no ambitious views excited to the prejudice of that station in which Providence has placed them, the exercise of the scholars is restrained to reading in the Old and New Testament, and to spelling as a preparative for it.

The utility of Sunday Schools has been the subject of much conversation and debate. An appeal to facts may at once determine the point in question. The Committee of the Sunday School Society therefore beg to submit to the perusal of the public, the following extracts from letters which they have received, among many others from different parts of the kingdom.

The Society have no cause to complain of want of attention to their plan. The instruction afforded to nearly fifty thousand poor persons, in less than five years, having exceeded their most sanguine expectations. But while they congratulate themselves and the public on such an extension of the institution, they are constrained by the present state of their plans to make a fresh appeal to you, and through you to such of your friends as may be likely to patronize a design which has perhaps a superior claim upon the humane and benevolent to any other establishment—for, not to detract from the merit of other charities, which open sources of consolation for present suffering, not to arraign the wisdom of laws made for the punishment of crimes, this proceeds on the more enlarged and truly political principle of endeavoring to prevent them.

Sensible of the advantages the community must derive from the institution, the Society feel great concern in being under the necessity of adding that their expenses have lately much exceeded their receipts. The applications for assistance are numerous, and it would give pain to refuse them when sanctioned by proper recommendations. On your exertions, therefore, and those of a generous public, they depend for the completion of a reform so happily begun, and in which mankind are so deeply interested.

By order of the Committee.

HENRY THORNTON, Chairman.

The letters from which the extracts referred to in the above circular were taken, were from different parts of the country—all giving thanks to the Society for the supply of books sent to the schools, and bearing testimony to the good effects of the schools in restraining crime, creating a desire for learning, and an increased regard for the religious observance of the Sabbath.

CHAPTER XI.

For the ensuing letter we are under obligations to the volume entitled, "Robert Raikes; his Sunday Schools and his Friends." It was written to an old friend, a lady in Chelsea, London. Although it is, in some respects, similar to others from his pen, yet we think it contains enough of new thoughts to repay a perusal. It was written at

Gloucester, Nov. 5, 1787.

My Dear Madam:—Amongst the numerous correspondents which my little project for civilizing the rising generation of the poor has led me to address, I have to no one taken up my pen with more pleasure than to you, my old friend, with whom I formerly passed so many cheerful hours.

I am rejoiced to find that the people in your neighborhood are thus ready to listen to that strong and pathetic injunction given by our Saviour, a little before His resurrection, [ascension], "Feed my lambs;" and if it were possible for me to afford any hints that might be useful, great would be the pleasure I should receive. In answer to your queries, I shall as concisely as possible state, that I endeavor to assemble the children as early as is consistent with their perfect cleanliness—an indispensable rule ; the hour prescribed in our rules is eight o'clock, but it is usually half after eight before our flock is collected. Twenty is the number allotted to each teacher ; the sexes [are] kept separate. The twenty are divided into four classes ; the children who show any superiority in attainments, are placed as leaders of the several classes, and employed in teaching the others their letters, or, in hearing them read in a low whisper, which may be done without interrupting the master or mistress in their business, and will keep the attention of the children engaged, that they do not play or make a noise. Their attending the services of the church once a day, has, to me, seemed sufficient, for their time may be spent more profitably, perhaps, in receiving instruction, than in being present at a long discourse, which their minds are not able yet to comprehend. But people may think differently on this point. Within this month the minister of my parish has at last condescended to give me assistance in this laborious work, which I have now carried on six years with little or no support. He chooses that the children should come to church both morning and afternoon. I brought them to church only in the afternoon. If this should answer better than my plans, on some future occasion I will let you or Mr. H. know it.

The stipend to the teachers here is a shilling each Sunday; but we find them firing [fuel], and bestow gratuities as rewards of diligence, which may make it worth sixpence more.

But the success of the whole depends on the attention paid by people of condition. If persons of some consequence will condescend to officiate as visitors, and by kind words encourage the good among these despised and hitherto neglected creatures, and give gentle reproof to those who stray from their duty, a wonderful effect will, in a few months, be discoverable. Were I among you, I would call forth the gentlemen to visit the boys, and the ladies to superintend the girls. * * * * * * * *

It had sometimes been a difficult task to keep the children in proper order when they were all assembled at church; but I now sit near them myself, which has had the effect of preserving the most proper decorum.

After the sermon in the morning, they return home to dinner, and meet at the Schools at half after one, and are dismissed at five, with strict injunctions to observe a quiet behaviour, free from all noise and clamor. Before the business is begun in the morning. they all kneel down, while a prayer is read, and the same before dismission in the evening.

To those children who distinguish themselves as ex-

amples of diligence, quietness in behaviour, observance of order, kindness to their companions, etc., I give some little token of my regard, as a pair of shoes if they are barefooted ; and some who are very bare of apparel, I clothe. This I have been enabled to do, in many instances, through the liberal support given by my brothers in the city. By these means, I have acquired considerable ascendency over the minds of the children. * * * * * * *
The people tell me that they keep their children in more order by the threat of telling Mr. Raikes, than they could formerly with the most severe stripes.

It is that part of our Saviour's character which I aim at imitating—" He went about doing good." No one can form an idea what benefits he is capable of rendering to the community by the condescension of visiting the dwellings of the poor. You may remember the place without the South-gate, called Littleworth—it used to be the St. Giles of Gloucester. By going amongst those people, I have totally changed their manners. They vow at this time that the place is quite a heaven to what it used to be. Some of the vilest of the boys are now so exemplary in behavior, that I have taken one into my service. I mention this as an evidence of what may be done. But I fear I am growing too prolix, and that I shall cause you to repent the opening a correspondence with your old acquaintance. I must tell you that I am blessed with six excellent girls and two lovely boys. My eldest boy was born the very day that I made public to the world the scheme of Sunday Schools, in my paper of November 3, 1783. In four years' time, it has extended so rapidly, as now to include two hundred and fifty thousand children; it is increasing more and more. It reminds me of the grain of mustard seed.

Previous to 1792, a district committee auxiliary to the London Society, had been formed at Wareham, Dorset county, Isle of Purbeck. That committee had been so efficient in its labors, that the Executive Committee of the London Society thought it no more than justice to recognise them by a letter of approval, hence the following from the Chairman of the Society's Committee, to the Chairman of the District Committee:

LONDON, March 18, 1792.

SIR:—We think it incumbent upon us to express our acknowledgements for the accurate and very particular returns which you have made to us of the Schools in your district, which evince an attention to the objects of this Society, that must give pleasure to every friend and promoter of it; to you, it must be unnecessary to expatiate on the merits of an institution which you have yourselves so warmly espoused; but from the consideration that you and we are embarked in the same cause, have the same laudable object in pursuit, and are exercising the same zeal for its promotion, we are persuaded it must afford you some satisfaction to be informed that we continue to receive the most flattering testimonies of good effects that are produced by the Sunday Schools in many parts of the kingdoin where they have been established, and although it is apparent to discerning minds that very great and permanent advantages are already attained, yet we are convinced the full benefits of our efforts are not yet felt, but will break out with increasing splendor when the subjects of them come into active life, and excited by a profitable experience, shall exert themselves to perpetuate to their own children, the happy means from which they will have derived such abiding advantages.

It is with concern we mention that in some places this encouragement is yet wanting from the parents, and that they do not sufficiently attend to the voice of Providence, calling them to espouse with gratitude, and enforce with earnestness, those advantages for their offspring which will assuredly prove far more durable riches than they can obtain for them in this world. It has afforded us real pleasure to observe the exertions that have been made in the Isle of Purbeck, and we are happy to embrace the present opportunity of expressing to you, gentlemen, and through you to all the parties concerned, the great satisfaction it has afforded us, that not only our plans have been adopted by gentlemen of liberality in these parts, but that such a privilege has been so thankfully received by those parents who have lauably availed themselves of this important charity, and most effectually unswered the end of their benefactors. Nor can we, on this occasion omit, with affectionate solicitude, to wish it may be recommended to the children, to second the endeavors of their parents, by cheerfully embracing the means of instruction offered them by this and other similar societies, and by a regular attendance at the schools, and by exemplary behaviour and conduct, encourage others to follow their commendable example, in which we cannot but think that the influence of the church wardens and overseers in every parish, if properly exerted, would contribute much to forward the design, both with children and their parents.

We particularly entreat that our best thanks may be accepted by the parochial clergy, and other gentlemen of the Committee, who have paid great attention to the schools, to secure a useful superintendence of them, and for the regularity of the returns, from which we have derived much useful information. May the happy union of these exertions be long continued, and may you, gentlemen, and your posterity after you, experimentally feel the effects which will assuredly follow these your good works.

Henry Thornton, Chairman.

The Society, it appears from the annual reports, continued to increase from year to year, so that down to 1796 it had established and assisted one thousand and eighty-six schools, with sixty-nine thousand two hundred and twenty-two scholars. It had distributed five thousand seven hundred and forty-nine Bibles, twenty-six thousand three hundred and twenty-one Testaments, and one hundred and ten thousand three hundred and eighty nine spelling books.

In the year 1798, an event took place in the his tory of the Society, which has led to consequences the most important in regard to the circulation of the Scriptures.

As early as 1789, Sunday Schools were introduced into the principality of Wales. Previous to that time the Bible in the Welsh language was in the houses of but few of the poor people. In some parishes not more than ten persons could read it. The only means of public instruction being circulating schools established by a few benevolent persons. These schools, after a few months' sojourn in one locality, would move to another, so that advancement under their care was slow and uncertain.

The introduction of Sunday Schools gave a new impetus to mental improvement, causing a demand for the Scriptures. The Rev. Thomas Charles, an Episcopal minister of Bala, Merionethshire, North Wales, had been a warm friend and supporter of Sunday

Schools from the beginning. He was the mover of the important measures alluded to as having occurred in 1798. In the latter part of that year, he was in London, and applied to the Executive Committee of the Sunday School Society for aid for the Sunday Schools already established in Wales, and for sending them to places not yet penetrated by them. As the funds of the society were raised for England only, his request could not be granted, but a separate fund was at once raised for Wales, and three thousand books, including Bibles and Testaments, were placed at the disposal of Mr. Charles. A letter from him, dated June 18, 1799, and published in the proceedings of the Society for that year, shows that the news of the English bounty " was received with great joy, and soon spread throughout the whole country."

He further savs—" Those who have been to the school six months, can in general read the Bible well."

The effect of this call upon the Society for aid, led the Executive Committee, in July, 1799, to inform the Society of their intention, if possible, to publish an edition of the New Testament in the Welsh language, " a measure which we have much at heart, being convinced of its great propriety and necessity, that the knowledge which has been acquired in Sunday Schools might be directed to the Scriptures, which are of infinite importance to the bodies and souls of men."

The Welsh people having learned that the Society were about making an effort to publish the Testament in their own language for their Sunday Schools, Mr. Charles speaks of the effect of that news, in a letter dated Bala, Jan. 13, 1800. He says :—"The report of the new edition of the Welsh Bible, [Testament,] has enlivened them much, especially as they are to be disposed of at so low a price. I am convinced of it, that five thousand Bibles could be immediately disposed of in North Wales, if they could be obtained. I know several districts without a Bible in all the families who live in them, and there was not an individual that could read among them till our schools were introduced. Now, being taught to read, like hungry persons, they are are ready to famish for want of Bibles. In some parts the Sunday Schools flourish more than ever, and beyond all dispute, do abundant good. I am convinced that hundreds of our poor children are preparing in them for useful stations in the church on earth, and in that above. What greater blessing can we look for ?"

From all we can learn of this subject, it appears that the Executive Committee, after having purchased the first 3,000 books, including Bibles and Testaments, were unable to publish the edition of the New Testament in the Welsh language, consequently, the hopes of the people were doomed to end in disappointment for the time being. This discussion of the subject, however, led to the accomplishment of the desired object by other means. Before proceeding to notice the means by which the Scriptures were supplied to the Welsh people, I will relate some incidents to show how great the destitution was. It is said that in the year 1802, as Mr. Charles was walking through the streets of Bala, he met a little girl who attended his ministry, and as he always had a word for children, he inquired if she could repeat the text, from which he had preached on the previous Sabbath. She not answering promptly, he repeated the inquiry. At length, she answered, "The weather has been so bad, that I could not get out to read the Bible." Upon further questioning her, he found the reason why she could not repeat the text was, there was no copy of the Scriptures to which she could gain access, either at her own home, or among her friends near, and she was accustomed to walk seven miles over the hills every week to where she could obtain a Welsh Bible, for the purpose of reading the chapter from which the minister took his text. It was a practice among the peasants for a number of families to unite in purchasing a Bible, and then circulate it among themselves as they might previously agree. An incident is related of twelve of these Welsh peasants subscribing together to purchase a copy of the Bible :—" Each family was to keep it a month and then pass it forward. On its arrival among them, an old man who had been the last subscriber, finding his name at the end of the list, wept bitterly, saying, 'Alas! it will be twelve months before it comes to me, and I dare say I shall be gone before that time into another world.'"

It was in this year, (1802), that Mr. Charles, ever mindful of the wants of his people, stated to the Executive Committee of the Religious Tract Society, how destitute they were of the Bible in their own language. He said, as they could not be obtained in the usual channels, it was desirable that "new and extraordinary means" be resorted to. This proposition gave rise to a conversation of some length, in the course of which, it was suggested by the Rev. J. Hughes, a Baptist minister, that as Wales was not the only part of the kingdom in which such a want might be supposed to prevail, it would be desirable to take such steps as might be likely to stir up the public mind to a general dissemination of the Scriptures.

This suggestion was warmly received by the rest of the company, and it expanded, by time and progressive discussion, until it culminated in the proposal and establishment of the British and Foreign Bible Society, in the year 1804. Its Executive Committee was formed in the same manner as that of the Sunday School Society, namely, one-half being members of the established church, and the other half dissenters.

CHAPTER XII.

THE reader remembers, no doubt, that the annual report of the Sunday School Society for 1788, showed that the Society had fifteen hundred pounds, or seven thousand five hundred dollars, invested in stocks drawing four per cent. interest. Nothwithstanding the organization and early working of the Society was, at the time, one of the grandest progressive movements on record, the tendency manifested to accumulate and invest funds increased with its age, until it fell somewhat behind the spirit of the times. The people were awakened to the importance of Sabbath Schools, and were not in a temper to be hampered by plodding machinery It is true, there were forcible apologies for the Society falling into this cautious way of doing business. The expense of conducting schools was much greater then than now. One single item, that of paid teachers alone, cost them from 1785 to 1800, not less than twenty thousand dollars, and, like all other business in which money has a place in its system, with the demand for teachers, the claims for remuneration increased.

But, by degrees, gratuitous teachers were raised up, and in a few schools, such as Stockport, hired teachers were early dispensed with. I am not informed of a single instance where the plan of gratuitous teaching was tried, that they returned to the pay system. This movement for gratuitous teaching was not confined to any particular man or locality, but as one who might be called an evangelist in the cause of free teaching, was intimately connected with another important movement, I will give a short sketch of his early life :

* " William Brodie Gurney was born at Camberwell, near, London, in December, 1777, and was connected with a family who have long been, and still are, employed by the British Government as stenographic writers, by which an ample income has been secured. When William was about ten years old, he thus speaks of himself:—' I was occasionally sent, by my mother, to inquire after the health of Mr. Hensham, a superannuated Independent [Congregational] minister, who resided at Kingsland, in the house of Mr. William Fox, [founder of the Sunday School Society] ; and frequently, while I trundled my hoop, I took on my left arm a little basket with some jelly, or a little

* Am. Bap. Pub. Soc.

cake, refreshments which he had not the means of purchasing, his income being very small, and he having refused assistance, which was generously offered him by Mr. Whitbread [a liberal member of Parliament], and from Mr. Howard, both of whom felt a great esteem for him. On one of these occasions, I found an elderly gentleman, whose figure I still bear in my mind, as well as his dress, a pepper and salt [colored] coat, and a scarlet waistcoat, and lying by him a cocked hat. That was John Howard, the philanthropist."

About this time [1787] Mr. Gurney removed with his father's family to Walworth, then an adjoining village to Camberwell, but the whole neighborhood is now included in mighty London. Before he was united with the Baptist church at Mazepond, which was in 1796, when he was but nineteen years of age, he began to be active in the cause of Christ. In the neighborhood of his father's house at Walworth was a school which had been raised by the efforts of his mother. The master was encouraged by the Committee for its support to open it on Sunday for religious instruction, and was rewarded with a penny, or two cents a child, for each Sunday up to the number of thirty. "Feeling a desire," says Mr. Gurney, "to be of some use, I determined to visit the Sunday School, and I very soon ascertained that the attendance was uniformly the same. If the thirty did not make their appearance, the master's son was sent to fetch in the requisite number, who were informed that they would not be detained. I found that they were learning very little, and doubted whether the school was doing any good. It was in vain I reasoned with the master on the facility of doubling the numbers; and soon concluded that the only method of rendering the school useful was to take it out of the hands of the master. Gratuitous instruction had been commenced in some places near London, but there was a strong feeling against it. Having, however, conferred with three friends, we offered ourselves to the Committee as willing to undertake the management of the Sunday instruction, and obtained their consent. Having hired a separate room, we canvassed the neighborhood for scholars, and in a few weeks had a school of one hundred and twenty children."

The result of these efforts was to convince all who saw them that the voluntary system of instruction by those whose hearts were interested in the welfare of the children was the only true way of conducting Sunday Schools. In consequence of this conviction many other schools were formed within three years by Mr. Gurney and his friends, and a schoolhouse erected for their accommodation, with a general extension of their plans. All this was done independently of the old Society, Mr. Gurney having raised nearly all the money by his own personal appeals.

There does not seem to have been any intention in

the outset to get up a new organization; but as the old Society represented the idea of paid teachers, they were often led to employ those whose modes of instruction were somewhat antiquated — consequently did not possess that vivacity and life so indispensable in the instruction of children.

Those young men volunteered their services because their hearts were in the work; and after having sustained themselves three years with increased interest, their warm and sympathetic feelings naturally drew them together, and they found in conversation that by friendly discussion their zeal in the cause might be strengthened, and their plans of instruction improved.

In the early part of 1803 Mr. Gurney removed to the western portion of London, and his house became the general resort of the friends of the Sunday School cause in that part of the city. It was after this removal that he suggested to the Sunday School teachers of London, that it might be to their mutual advantage, and for the good of the cause, for them to unite to discuss their plans of operation, and as far as possible extend them over the world. The Rev. Rowland Hill was then pastor of Surrey Chapel, a Calvinistic Methodist house of worship. Mr. Hill threw open the schoolrooms of his chapel, and on July 13, 1803, the London Sunday School Union was organized. Of this institution Mr. Gurney was as truly the founder as Mr. Fox was of the Sunday School Society, and he was successively its Secretary, Treasurer, and President.

In every way the Sunday School Union was successful. It held quarterly meetings in its four different London auxiliaries, for devotional exercises and the discussion of practical questions—appropriated considerable sums for establishing schools at home and abroad—and published Sunday School books, periodicals and papers. It is yet vigorously doing the work that it commenced so long ago. One of the curiosities connected with its early history was the holding of an early breakfast in connection with its anniversary meeting.

And it is said one of the most useful results of this Union was to infuse new life into the old Sunday School Society. It was mentioned a few pages back, that this Society was not acting in harmony with the progressive spirit of the times. Mr. Gurney, always an active working man, was at one time put forward by a number of friends of the same spirit, rather reluctantly on his part, as a manager or member of the Executive Committee. He was elected at a public meeting over considerable opposition from the "old fogy" party. His advent into the management of the Society gave new energy to its movements.

Many years after, the pressure of other engagements prevented him from attending regularly the business meetings. Taking advantage of this, the managers resorted to their old plans of investing the funds of the Society in public stocks, having accumulated many thousand pounds in this way. Mr. Gurney thought it wrong thus to withhold it from the legitimate purpose for which it was intended by the donors.

He went to the editor of a periodical called the "Revivalist," that paper having an extensive circulation among Sunday School teachers, and expressed an earnest desire to the editor that the treasury of the Society should be exhausted. The editor entertaining similar views and feelings, announced in the next number of his paper that the Sunday School Society was possessed of ample wealth, and urged on all the poor Sunday Schools throughout the British dominions, and all others who were disposed to organize such institutions, to apply to them for aid.

It is said that no small amusement was afforded to outsiders by the complaints of the managers at their frequent calls to read letters of application for aid, to grant books, &c. Their funds, too, that they had felt were so snugly invested, afforded them considerable uneasiness as they saw them passing away, forgetting that they were intended for these very channels.

Their feelings towards Mr. Gurney for his statement to the editor of the Revivalist, also against the editor for the commotion he had excited, were not the most amiable—but those two gentlemen bore it patiently, satisfied that their object was accomplished, hundreds of new Sabbath Schools having been organized, and many others increased in their efficiency.

In 1805 the Executive Committee of the Sunday School Society reported that from the organization of the Society, twenty years previous, they had granted to schools needing pecuniary assistance the sum of four thousand one hundred and forty-seven pounds, eight shillings and five pence; they had established and assisted two thousand five hundred and forty-two schools, containing two hundred and twenty-six thousand nine hundred and forty-five pupils; had donated two hundred and nineteen thousand four hundred and ten spelling books, fifty thousand one hundred and twenty-six copies of the New Testament, and seven thousand two hundred and thirteen copies of the Bible.

The early movement for gratuitous teachers gained such strength that in 1794, of thirty employed in the Stockport schools, twenty-four were rendering their services free. This proportion did not prevail in other places—but as we have already seen, a few young men starting out with that idea, embodied it in the organization of the London Sunday School Union in 1803. All these influences were brought to bear upon the old Society, and by the year 1805 gratuitous teaching prevailed in nearly or quite all the schools—

hence we find that in their proceedings of that year, they decided that as the Society was without any permanent income except about five hundred pounds, they would not longer continue the practice of paying teachers.

Sunday Schools had been introduced into Ireland in a few places not long after their commencement in England, but there was no effort for their general introduction until 1809. In November of that year a Sunday School Society was formed for Ireland. Its objects were stated to be similar to others organized for the same purpose, except that they paid no attention to the internal management of the schools. The only connection between the schools and the Society being for the latter to supply spelling books and Scriptures gratuitously, or at reduced prices.

In Lloyd's Life of Raikes there is a table showing the number of schools and scholars under the care of the Irish Society at each annual report from the first to 1825. The first report in 1810 shows that the Society had two schools and eighty-seven scholars. In 1825 it had one thousand seven hundred and two schools, and one hundred and fifty thousand eight hundred and thirty-one scholars.

There was another Society for Ireland called the London Hibernian Society, which reported in the same year, seventeen thousand one hundred and forty-five scholars.

There seems to have been a necessity for schools, where persons with families, or in middle age, who had not learned to read when young, might have an opportunity to do so without being embarrassed by the presence of children. A History of these schools, written by Dr. Pole, an eminent physician and a member of the Society of Friends, was published in England some years ago. Never having been able to procure a copy of it, or any other on the same subject, my information is mostly in fragments. Many adults had, from nearly the commencement of Sunday Schools, attended with the children—but many others who were in need of such instruction, would stay away rather than place themselves in such embarrassing positions. So far as I am informed, all parties award to the Rev. Thomas Charles the honor of having commenced the first Sunday School for adults, at Bala, North Wales, in the summer of 1811. He says in a letter to the Secretary of the Hampshire Sydney Sunday School Union, dated April 12, 1812—

"Observing and bewailing the great number of the illiterate grown-up and old people in our poor country, I have in different places published Sunday Schools exclusively for them, having another in the same place for children—telling them at the same time that we meant to be urgent upon them, never ceasing to press them to attend until they came. By kindness and importunity we have succeeded far beyond our most sanguine hopes. We have six of these schools for the aged set up within these three or four months, and some hundreds have learned and are learning to read. By condescension, kindness and patience they have been engaged to learn, and their desire for learning soon became as great as any we have seen among the young people. They have their little elementary books with them often whilst at work, and meet in the evenings, of their own accord, to teach one another. The rumor of the success of these schools has spread abroad, and has greatly removed the discouragement which old people felt from attempting to learn at their age. This has been practically proved to be false, for old people of seventy-five years of age have learned to read in these schools, to their great comfort and joy. I dare not vouch positively for the conversion of any of them; but I can say, that they are much improved in their moral conduct and attendance on the means of grace. They lament with tears their former ignorance, and rejoice they can read, and repeat *memoriter* a few verses of the Bible given them to learn. In some degree their blind minds are enlightened, and their hearts are impressed by divine truths, until they are generally melted to tears of joy, mixed with sorrow. Pray for them.

"I began these schools for five aged in my own neighborhood, but mean to drive them on, and set them up in all parts of the country as soon as I possibly can. I am happy to inform you also for your encouragement, that in several districts very great, powerful and general awakenings have broken out, since the beginning of last winter, among the children and young people attending the Sunday Schools. Above one hundred and forty have joined one Society within these three months past. I visited them last month ; a hundred on a week-day met me to be publicly catechised. They are of all ages, from five to thirty, and their number is so great as to include nearly all the young people in the district. I catechised them before all the country, and their responses in every instance were scriptural and intelligent, always confirmed by a passage of Scripture. I did not confine myself to one subject only, but asked them questions upon every subject of importance in the Christian religion, to see whether they had obtained a clear, connected view of them—and in every instance I was highly satisfied. Their appearance was solemn and serious, often much affected. The work goes on there, not like tugging and rowing a fleet in dead waters, but like a ship sailing in full tide, with all her sails set, and the wind powerfully filling them.—My own mind experienced such impressions whilst among them as can never be obliterated. I thought it more than abundant recompense for all my labors these twenty-six years past in endeavoring to instruct the young people of our poor country. Not unto us, not unto us, but to thy name, O Lord, be all the glory."

In a letter to Dr. Pole, dated Jan. 4, 1814, Mr. Charles says :—

"In one county, after a public address had been delivered to them on that subject, the adult poor, even the aged, flocked to Sunday Schools in crowds; and the shop-keepers could not immediately supply them with an adequate number of spectacles. Our schools, in general, are kept in our chapels; in some districts, where there are no chapels, farmers, in the summer time, lend their barns. The adults and children are sometimes in the same room, but placed in different parts of it. When their attention is gained and fixed, they soon learn; their age makes no difference, if they are able, by the help of glasses, to see the letters. As the adults have no time to lose, we endeavor, before they can read, to instruct them without delay, in the first principles of Christianity. We select a short portion of Scripture, comrpising in plain terms the leading doctrines, and repeat them to the learners till they can retain them in their memories; and which they are to repeat the next time we meet. It is impossible for me, at present, to ascertain the number of adults in the schools; in many districts they all attend, and the beneficial results of them are everywhere observed."

At the second anniversary of the Bristol Auxiliary Bible Society, a letter was read from Keynsham, a neighboring village, which said:

"We have been necessarily obliged to omit a great number of poor inhabitants who could not read, and therefore are not likely to be benefitted by the possession of a Biblo." A man in humble circumstances named William Smith, hearing this statement, his benevolent mind meditated upon their situation, and alternating between hope and fear, he consulted Stephen Prust, Esq., a merchant of Bristol who had already acquired a reputation for philanthropy. Mr. Smith desired to know whether it was possible to instruct adults to read. Mr. Prust gave him every encouragement, and promised assistance, and in nineteen days after their first interview on the subject, a school was opened with eleven men and ten women. In 1813 a society was formed in Bristol to spread these adult schools. Dr. Pole, whom I have spoken of as their historian, is mentioned as one of the most efficient laborers in this cause.

Similar Societies were formed in other parts of the country. In a report of the Gainesborough Adult School Society, it is stated that—"An old woman ninety-four years of age, at Ipswick work-house, made better progress without spectacles than some of the younger people, some of whom she undertook to teach. A woman ninety-eight years old at Manchester, went to a boys' school and received instruction; she reads aloud in the school. In Gloucestershire an old man is mentioned who had been immoral all his early life, learning to read at eighty years of age, and his wife at seventy. The old gentleman said the Scripture verses gave him great comfort when lying awake at night."

These schools penetrated also into Ireland; a communication from there speaking of them says:—

"In a village where lately the Scriptures were unknown, I found a venerable man nearly one hundred years old, with a Bible in his hand, and many of his neighbors, who, after their labor, had come to hear him read. Two grandchildren were at his knee teaching him. They would occasionally correct him, saying, 'Stop, grandfather, that is not the right word, there is the word.'"

In Scotland also they were found. At Glenclavie on one of the islands of Scotland it is said the people flocked in crowds to the schools. An old soldier named Iverich, one hundred and seventeen years old, says he entered the army in 1715, and the Sunday School in 1815. After learning the alphabet, and to connect monosyllables, his sight failed, and he could go no further. It is only proper to say that these schools were formed for adults, not for the very old.

CHAPTER XIII.

For nearly thirty years, Mr. Raikes was permitted to witness the extension of Sunday Schools, and he was humbly thankful that the Divine blessing had so remarkably attended those unpretending seminaries, for the establishment of which he had so faithfully and perseveringly labored. In the year 1809, Mr. Raikes' health began to fail, and continued to decline until April 5, 1811, when his life terminated suddenly. He was not thought to be in danger, but experiencing a oppression on his chest, a physician was called immediately, who declared his case hopeless, and in a little more than half an hour he was a corpse. He died in his native city. He came to his grave in full age, as a sheaf of wheat ready for the garner, and we have reason to believe that the Saviour, for whom he had so faithfully labored in life, did not forsake him in death. His remains were deposited in the south aisle of the ancient church of St. Mary de Crypt, in the city of Gloucester.

The following inscription in Latin is placed on the tomb erected to his parents and himself.

M. S.
ROBERTI RAIKES
In haec civitate nuper Typographi
Qui obiit die Septem. 7th
Anno { Salutis 1757
Ætatis suæ 68 }

Uxoris item optimae
MARIAE Revd. Ricardi Drew
filoe
Qui obiit die Octbr. 30th
Anno { Salutis 1779
Ætatis suæ 65 }

ROBERTI etiam horum Filii natu maximi
Qui Scholis Sabbaticis hic primum a se institutis
nec non apud alios
Felici opera studioque sub commendatis
Obiit die April 5
Anno { Salutis 1811
Ætatis suæ 75 }

TRANSLATION OF THE EPITAPH.

Sacred to the Memory
of
ROBERT RAIKES
Late Printer in this City
Who departed this life on the 7th day of September
In the year { of our Salvation 1757
of his age 68 }

Also of
MARIA his beloved wife daughter of the Rev Richard Drew
who died the 30th October
In the year { of our Salvation 1811
of her age 65 }

Also of
ROBERT
Their eldest son
By whom Sabbath Schools were first instituted in this Place
and were also
By his successful exertion and assiduity
Recommended to others
He died on the 5th day of April
In the year { of our salvation 1811
of his age 75 }

The Saviour said, "They that take the sword shall perish with the sword." Although this declaration has gone forth from him who spoke nothing but truth, men in all ages have erected the most splendid mausoleums to those who have been most successful in leading armies of human beings to the slaughter of each other, while those who have been the greatest benefactors to their race in deeds of peace, have often been permitted to pass from the scenes of their earthly labors without a stone to mark the place where their bodies were deposited.

Should the reader wish to see a monument to Raikes, he need not make a pilgrimage to the place where his ashes are enshrined, to read the inscription just quoted as a memento, that he lived to bless the world. It matters not upon what part of the civilized globe you are, you have only to visit the nearest place of worship, on a Sabbath morning, to find in the Sunday School the most durable cenotaph ever erected to man; durable, because susceptible of reproducing itself, as it has long since been demonstrated that those who enter these schools as pupils make the most efficient teachers and superintendents.

It has fallen to the lot of the city of Gloucester to witness the extremes of degradation and virtue, of barbarism and civilization, in the martyrdom of Bishop Hooper,* and the establishment of Sunday Schools.

* John Hooper was born in Somersetshire, about the year 1495: he was educated at Oxford, afterwards joined the frater-

Gloucester was not to blame for this atrocious act, the power there manifested emanated from the seat of government. Had that city been culpable, however, the establishment of Sunday Schools would, to some extent, have atoned for the inhuman act.

It would seem almost incredible that these schools, after having, by the aid of various societies, extended themselves into almost every country of the civilized world, actually ceased to exist in their native city a short time before the death of their founder. Such was the case, and there seemed to be but little anxiety on the part of the citizens to have them revived. From Watson's history of the Sunday School Union, we learn that the schools were extinct previous to 1780, and about that time six pious young men, who had realized their value, united and resolved, by the

nity of Cistercian monks, but disliking their principles, returned to the doctrines of Luther. For this he was prosecuted, and after several very narrow escapes in England, France, and Ireland, fled to Switzerland, and there married. On the death of Henry VIII, in 1547, he returned to London, and during the reign of Edward VI, became a popular preacher, and was made Bishop of Gloucester in 1550. Upon the death of Edward, in 1553, and the accession to the throne of his sister, the bloody Mary, Bishop Hooper was marked for destruction. He was condemned to be burned, and the sentence was executed in the city of Gloucester, in 1555. His death afforded the strongest testimony that could have been given of his faith in the doctrines of the Christian religion.

aid of their Master, to revive the work in its birthplace. They applied to their Pastor for his approval and co-operation. His reply was—" No, the children will make too much noise." They then applied to the officers of the Church ; their answer was—" No, the children will soil the place so that we cannot let you have it." They then appealed to the lay members of the church, but without the least encouragement ; their objection being more than both the others ; they said —" No, you will find no children, no teachers, and no money to pay expenses."

But these young men were possessed of too much of the revival spirit thus to be foiled. " They met around a post, at the corner of a lane, within twenty yards of the spot where Bishop Hooper was burned alive more than two hundred and fifty years before, and there, taking each other by the hand, they solemnly resolved that, come what would, Sunday Schools should be re-established in the city of Gloucester."

These young men were only able to raise about three dollars and fifty cents, and with that they commenced their schools. How they succeeded we are unable to say, but feel quite satisfied that should they again become extinct there, the friends of Sabbath Schools throughout the world, would regard their Mecca as missionary ground, and act accordingly.

In the Amercan Sunday School Magazine, for Jan.,

1826, there is an article on the life of Raikes, which contains some quotations from a writer over the initials J. J. He was a Sunday School teacher, and was traveling on mercantile business through the west of England; he made it convenient to spend a few days in the city of Gloucester. While there he took a sketch of the monumental tablet, and copied the inscription already given. He also composed the following lines while viewing the tomb, and meditating on the effects of his labors as the Founder of Sunday Schools:

"Spirit of Charity! which guided Raikes,
Guide thou me, to emulate his deeds.
May I inspired by this sweet sacred hour,
Be led to pray for sovereign grace to aid
My humble efforts in the same good cause,
Esteeming it delightful to succeed
The steps of one--his country's benefactor,—
Who, as a friend of youth and Sabbath Schools,
Now shines resplendent as a star in heaven.
O, may my fellow-teachers, with myself,
Desire and feel his pure philanthropy,
His energetic interest for the poor;
And having pledged ourselves to work,
In leading poverty's neglected babes,
To find an entrance to eternal joys.
Here would we pause a while o'er Raikes' tomb,
Till memory ranges all his worthiest deeds,
And bids succeeding teachers imitate!"

In answer to inquiries, I have received, among many others, the two following notes, from the Mayor of Gloucester, and from Henry Raikes, Esq., Registrar of Chester, England. They were both accompanied by valuable documents from authentic sources. From these papers I glean the principal facts concerning Mr. Raike's family. Among the papers from the Mayor, was that copied in the second chapter, giving the genealogy of the Raikes family for three hundred and fifty years.

GLOUCESTER, Nov. 30, 1858.

SIR—As Mayor of Gloucester, the above communications have been sent to me, of which, to save expense, I have had copies made. I trust these communications may answer your purpose.

I am, Sir,
Your obedient servant,
RICH'D. HELPS.

J. C. Power.

CHESTER REGISTRY, Nov. 19, 1858.

SIR—Partly from my own family knowledge, and partly from the recollections of Mrs. Ladbroke, the only surviving child of Mr. Robert Raikes, who was my great uncle, I am able to furnish you with the following particulars which I think comprise all you want to know of the domestic relations, and incidents of the founder of Sunday Schools.

I am, sir,

Yours truly,

H. RAIKES.

J. C. Power.

The writer of the last letter is a grandson of Thomas Raikes, a brother to the founder of Sunday Schools. Mr. Raikes the philanthropist was married but once; the different authorities conflict with regard to the date of his marriage—one near relation says 1763, Burke the historian says 1767, and the writer of the above note says 1772. It is strange that there is such discrepancy about it, but I give them all that the reader may judge, where I am unable to decide, and that the descendants may have an opportunity to correct the error.

They also conflict with regard to the number of his children—some say he had two sons and three daughters, others two sons and six daughters. The latter is undoubtedly correct, being confirmed by himself in his letter of Nov. 5, 1787, found in the eleventh chapter. His wife and all his children survived him. His eldest son, the Rev. Robert Raikes, [called in some places Robert Napier Raikes,] Vicar of Longhope, in Gloucestershire, married Miss Caroline Probyn, daughter of the venerable Archdeacon Probyn. He had a number of children, the eldest of whom is named Robert Napier Raikes—he is the present representative of the family, is Colonel of a cavalry regiment in India, and has been distinguished as an efficient officer in suppressing the late sepoy mutiny.

William Raikes, the second son of the philanthropist, was a Colonel in the Coldstream Guards. He distinguished himself in the Peninsular war, after which he married a daughter of Lord Henley and died without issue.

Anne Raikes, the eldest daughter, married Sir Thomas Boulden Thompson, Baronet.

Mary, the second daughter, married Admiral Sir Thomas Thompson, who lost a leg at Copenhagen, under Lord Nelson, and died Governor of Greenwich Hospital. They left a number of children.

Albina, the third daughter, married John Birch, Esq.

Eleanor, the fourth daughter, married Daniel Garnett, Esq.

Charlotte, the fifth daughter, married William Stanley Clarke, Esq., who was a director of the East India Company, and commander of the naval forces in the East. When in command of a fleet of merchantmen he was attacked by a squadron of French pirates, but succeeded in bringing his ships and cargo safe to England—and for this he was knighted Sir William Stanley Clarke, presented with a sword by the city of London, and with a service of plate by the East India Company. He left a large family, part of whom are in India.

Caroline, the sixth daughter, married James Weller Ladbroke, Esq. She has one daughter, married to the Rev. H. D. Clarke. Mrs. Ladbroke was living in 1858, the only surviving child of Robert Raikes. She furnished much of this information to H. Raikes, Esq., of Chester, who forwarded it to me as previously stated.

One of my English correspondents, speaking of the four brothers of the founder of Sunday Schools, says, "Thomas Raikes, grandfather of H. Raikes, Esq., of Chester, was Governor of the Bank of England, and a very wealthy merchant—the personal friend of Mr. Pitt, and his adviser in many financial matters. His son Henry was Chancellor of Chester, and another—George—a director of the India Company. Two of his daughters married—the one Lord William Fitzroy, the other Lord Stratford de Radcliffe, the eminent ambassador, formerly known as Sir S. Canning, the Minister of England to the United States of America.

William Raikes, another brother [of the philanthropist] was a merchant and banker of Hull, and left a large fortune to his sons.

Charles Raikes was a wine merchant of London, and died rich without issue.

Rev. Richard Raikes, a most learned and pious man, graduated with the highest honors at Cambridge, and died a Canon of St. Davies, and a clergyman in the city of Gloucester ; married, but without issue.

The following is related of Robert Raikes by Mrs. Raikes, of Cheltenham, England.

"Mr. Raikes' philanthropy was universal—he was a constant visiter in the prisons at Gloucester, and took an especial interest in the spiritual welfare of the convicts. One case is particularly remembered by his only daughter.

"The Judges always dined one day with Mr. Raikes during the Assizes at Gloucester, and upon one of these occasions he took the opportunity of bringing before the Judge the case of a felon who had been condemned to death that morning for sheep-stealing, and earnestly entreated that the man's life should be spared.

"The Judge at first refused to listen to the petition on the ground that he was an old offender, and that the law must take its course. Mr. Raikes replied he knew the man had been a very wicked fellow, but that he now believed him to be a most sincere penitent. The Judge then replied, 'Well, Mr. Raikes, I am sure we are much indebted to you for the pains you have taken with poor criminals, and I will grant the request you so much desire, and give you the man—but he must be transported for life to Botany Bay.'

Mr. Raikes said, 'That quite satisfies me.' The sheep-stealer was accordingly sent to Botany Bay, where his conduct was so exemplary that in the course of a few years he was released from all future punishment and confinement in the colonies, and established a Sunday School of his own at Botany Bay. He was in correspondence with Mr. Raikes till within a few years of his death."

Only contemplate! The laws of a Christian nation putting a man to death for stealing a sheep to save himself and family from starving, and at the same time permit MAN-stealers to assist in making the laws—which was literally true of England and America at that time. But, thank God, this has long since ceased to be the case in England, and we have every reason to hope that its end is at hand in America, and that man-stealers and slave-drivers will never more legislate for us.

The following incident narrated by Mr. Raikes himself will give an idea of the esteem in which he was held by those who received the benefit of his instructions, and at the same time illustrate the fact that wicked parents may be reclaimed through the agency of their children when it could not be done in any other way. Mr Raikes says—

"One day as I was going to church, I overtook a soldier just entering the church door; this was on a week day. As I passed him, I said it gave me pleasure to see that he was going to a place of worship.—'Ah, sir,' said he, 'I may thank you for that.' 'Me!' said I—'why I do not know that I ever saw you before.' 'Sir,' said he, 'when I was a little boy I was indebted to you for my first instruction in my duty. I used to meet you at the morning service in this cathedral, and was one of your Sunday scholars. My father, when he left this city, took me into Berkshire, and put me apprentice to a shoemaker. I used often to think of you. At length I went to London, and was there drawn to serve as a milita-man in the Westminster militia. I came to Gloucester last night with [in charge of] a deserter, and took the opportunity of coming this morning to visit the old spot, and in hopes of once more seeing you.' He then told me his name, and brought himself to my recollection by a curious circumstance which happened whilst he was at school. His father was a journeyman currier, a most vile and profligate man. After the boy had been some time at school, he came one day and told me that his father was wonderfully changed, and that he had left off going to the ale-house on Sunday. It happened soon after that I met the man in the street, and said to him, 'My friend, it gives me great pleasure to hear that you have left off going to the ale-house on the Sunday—your boy tells me that you now stay at home and never get tipsy.' 'Sir,' said he, 'I may thank you for it.' 'Nay,' said I, 'that is impossible

—I do not recollect that I ever spoke to you before.' ' No, sir,' said he, ' but the good instructions you give my boy, he brings home to me—and it is that, sir, which has induced me to reform my life.' "

Another fact may be adduced to show that he left no means untried to impress the duty of obedienoo to parents on the minds of children however humiliating it might be to himself,—the circumstance is related by Mr. Joseph Lancaster, who probably received it from Mr. Raikes.

It was his custom to visit the parents and children at their homes. He called upon a family one day, and found a little girl that had been disobedient—she was crying, and very stubborn. Her mother told Mr. Raikes she could do nothing with the girl. By her leave he commenced talking to the girl, and told her the first step in the right direction was to kneel before her mother and ask forgiveness for her disobedience.

The girl continued stubborn, when he said to her, " If you have no regard for yourself, I have much for you, and you will be ruined unless you learn to obey your parents—and if you will not humble yourself, I must do it for you." He then dropped upon his knees, and placing himself in an imploring attitude before the mother, began to ask in the most humble language her forgiveness. It had the desired effect—the real offender came at once to her feelings—she burst into tears, fell upon her knees and asked forgiveness—completely cured.

Mr. Lancaster, in referring to an interview he had with Mr. Raikes, says—"I was naturally desirous of gaining information and instruction from a venerable man of seventy-two, who had, in a series of years, superintended the education of three thousand poor children—who had been actively engaged in visiting both the city and county prisons, whereby he had gained an ample opportunity of knowing if any of the scholars were brought in as prisoners—and who on appealing to his memory, which although at an advanced age, is strong and lively, could answer, None !"

The same gentleman adds that Mr. Raikes has been heard to say—"I can never pass by the spot where the word 'TRY' came so powerfully into my mind, without lifting my hands and heart to heaven, in gratitude to God for having put such a thought into my heart."

Let me ask the reader to unite with me in resolving to TRY whenever an opportunity for doing good presents itself—and although we may not hope to accomplish as much as it was the privilege of Mr. Raikes to do, we shall doubtless many times have cause to be thankful that we made the effort.

I cannot close this memoir in a more appropriate manner than by quoting the lines of Tappan, describing the recruiting excursions of the founder of Sunday Schools in the suburbs of Gloucester.

"And who is he that's seeking,
With look and language mild,
To heal the heart that's breaking,
And glad the vagrant child?

"He searches lane and alley,
The mean and dark abode,
From Satan's hosts to rally,
The conscripts due to God,

"With words of kindly greeting,
Warm from an honest heart,
He's ignorance entreating,
In knowledge to have part.

"With Charity unfailing,
He patiently doth take
Rebuke and sinful railing,
For Christ, the Shepherd's sake.

"He wins from vicious mothers,
The children of neglect;
The sisters and the brothers,
From households sadly wrecked.

"And these, the truth impressing,
Beneath his gentle rule,
Have called on him a blessing,
Who formed the Sunday School.

" I'd rather my life's story,
  Should have such episode,
Than all the gorgeous glory
  Napoleon's history showed.

" For when no more war's banner,
  With shouting is unfurled,
Those children's sweet hosanna
  May shake the upper world."

CHAPTER XIV.

Having given the reader a history of the early part of the life of Mr. Fox in the third chapter, I shall now proceed to give an account of his last days.

In order to present a more connected view of the subject, I must go back and note the different changes of his place of residence, which have been quite frequent for an Englishman, especially one who resided all his life in England.

His birth-place, as we have already stated, was at the village of Clapton, in Gloucestershire, which is in the western part of England, near Wales. In the seventeenth year of his age, he commenced an apprenticeship as salesman in a mercer and draper establishment in the city of Oxford, situate east of Gloucester, between that place and London. He resided at Oxford about twelve years, having in the mean time risen from the position of an apprentice to that of proprietor. About 1764 he was married, and removed to London, where he was successfully engaged in mercantile pursuits for a period of twenty-three years.

It was during this time that he was enabled to accomplish the designs that have given him a prominent place on the roll of the benefactors of mankind. Finding his two sons, Jonathan and William, qualified to conduct his business, he gave it up to them in the year 1787, and removed to Donnyland near Colchester, the residence of his father-in-law, Mr. Tabor, be ing at the latter place. Colchester is situate northeast of London, in the county of Essex. This place proving unfavorable to the health of Mrs. Fox, they removed back to Islington near London, in 1789, and continued to reside there until 1799. Some years previous to this time, he had purchased the manor of his native village where his brother Samuel and Edward were still living, and near which resided a sister. He was not, however, permitted to make it his home ; the manor house being somewhat out of repair, he rented a country seat called Farmington Lodge, about four miles from Clapton. To this place he removed from Islington in 1799. About the year 1802 he left Farmington Lodge, and moved to Lechlade House in the south-eastern part of his native county. After his removal to Lechlade House, he never engaged in any active business, being then about sixty-six years of age. There were, however, many years in store for him, but he devoted the time to the entertainment of friends, and acts of charity. Before his removal to Lechlade, it is said that members of his own church suffered great persecution, but by his position in society, and his cordial co-operation with Christians of other denominations, those persecutions ceased and the prejudices against them were chiefly removed.

Mr. Fox presented the land on which to build a house of worship for the Baptist church at that place. The church edifice also being erected principally at his expense. He was chosen, at the organization of the church, to the same office he had held in London, namely, Deacon.

Although now quite advanced in age, Mr. Fox continued to correspond with his remaining fellow-laborers in the organization of the Sunday School Society. His zeal for the cause of religion, and his faith in all sufficiency of the Saviour were unabated, as will be seen by the following letter to Joseph Gutteridge, Esq., of Denmark Hill, in the suburbs of London.

LECHLADE HOUSE, June 29, 1809.

DEAR SIR:—I have somewhere read, and I was struck with the idea it was meant to convey, that harness not worn, is likely to become rusty. Indeed, I know a minister who, while he continued principally dependent for support on the work of the ministry, was thought to possess no inconsiderable abilities, but who, since his advancement in life by marriage, and having left off preaching, can hardly, if it be in a mixed company, find courage to ask a blessing on his food!

This perhaps, since there does not appear to be any decay of intellect, may be considered as a Divine judgment upon him.

And truly, my friend, the less I accustom myself to *write*, (and in this retired spot very little indeed occurs worth communicating), the more formidable letter-writing appears to me. I am not, however, at all disposed to give up a correspondent whose letters, though few in number, always afford me peculiar pleasure. As iron sharpeneth iron, so do the writings, as well as the countenance of a man his friend. They set me thinking, they bring to remembrance past occurrences, they cement friendships, and we know who hath said, "Thy own friend, and thy father's friend forsake thou not." Your letter carries my thoughts back to old times, when we walked to the house of God in company. They remind me of the company which we kept there, the business we transacted there, the preaching we heard there;—and what shall I say of the preacher? [the Rev. Abraham Booth, who died in 1806]. Oh, sir, it was indeed sometimes a pleasant season, and I am sometimes with you in spirit now; I go from pew to pew, I look at the attendants, some of them remain, while others have fallen asleep. I look at the pulpit, and what do I see? A good man no doubt, and a good preacher too, because you say so, but where is our friend ? I recognize his form in my imagination, but his bodily presence no longer cheers the eye, his voice no longer interests the mind, his work is finished, he is entered into his rest, his mantle however, still remains, and though dead, he yet speaketh. I sometimes look into his "Reign of Grace," and turn over others of his writings to catch, if possible, somewhat of the fire, to be animated with the same love and zeal, which shone so conspicuously throughout his whole life, but I fail. The object is not attained, and I go mourning for want of those ravishing joys, those Pisgah views, with which the people of God are sometimes visited on their way to glory. But God is gracious ; Christ is precious, Heaven is glorious, and grace is free. "I give unto my sheep," says our Lord, "eternal life, and they shall never perish, neither shall any man pluck them out of my hand." And what need we more, what better security can we ask or desire.

Mrs. Fox was greatly afflicted in the latter part of her life, notwithstanding which she was spared until February 5, 1823. She had been a consistent professor of religion for nearly eighty years. She was buried in the family vault, in the burial ground of the Chapel at Lechlade, where her daughter, Mrs. Mary Evill, had been buried only two years before.

The maiden name of Mrs. Tabor, the mother of

Mrs. Fox, was Grimstone; she was the lineal descendant of Sir H. Grimstone, a judge and member of Parliament in the latter part of the seventeenth century, during the reign of Charles the Second. He was a most devout Christian, and a wise and liberal statesman.

The ancestors of Mrs. Fox had always regarded feeding the hungry, and clothing the naked, as binding as any other duty. Therefore, they made it a custom on the return of every Sabbath, to supply some of the poor with a dinner, sent to them from their own table; to this practice, it is said *she constantly adhered;* and thus some who never tasted meat on other days, were sure of a comfortable meal on the Sabbath. She never, upon any occasion, turned a beggar away from her door unrelieved, and there were frequently many in the course of the day; her benevolence being known, she did not fail to have plenty of applicants—her idea was, better bestow on nine unworthy, than that one deserving object should want for a morsel of that bread which God had so bountifully given her.

After the death of her who had been his companion in youth, middle life, and old age, Mr. Fox removed from Lechlade, having spent twenty-one years there. His place of residence for the remainder of his days, was Cirencester, another village a few miles west of Lechlade, in the same county. As he was near ninety years of age, his correspondence of course must have been limited. Although there is a short quotation from the following letter in the third chapter, I feel like giving it entire in this place, as the last letter from him, and as evidence of his interest in Sunday Schools to the last. The letter is to the Rev. Dr. Newman, of Bow, and is dated:

CIRENCESTER, April 29, 1824.

DEAR SIR:—That no time should be lost, immediately on receipt of your letter, I forwarded your request with the magazine containing an account of our Sunday Schools, to my friend, Mr. B.; he, however, being confined by illness, did not attend the court of the company till lately, when the result of the business, I am sorry to say, proved unfavorable. And what shall we say to this? The importance of the object is not sufficiently considered, while a narrow and prejudiced spirit is too apparent, as it was in the chairman of our first meeting, who said, "Sir, I presume you intend to confine the plan to our own denomination, for then we shall go on in harmony." My answer was, "Sir, the work is great, and I shall not be satisfied until every person in the world be able to read the Bible, therefore we must call on all the world to help us." And its being thus made a general concern, paved the way for that noble institution the Bible Society, which found the people ready prepared to receive the sacred volume. I am sorry Mr. B.'s answer was delayed so long, he was himself friendly to the proposal.

I am, dear Sir,

Yours truly,

William Fox.

One of Mr. Fox's children, speaking of his latter days, says :—"Living as he did to the age of ninety, his memory, as may be supposed, failed him with regard to recent occurrences, but he would frequently dwell with the most minute exactness on the events of his childhood, as though they had occurred but yesterday."

"Under the pressure of trials that accumulated with his years, and which preyed upon his mind, I frequently turned his attention to those early scenes of his life which he loved so much to review. While conversing one day respecting his departed companion (my mother), he gave a very striking and affecting idea of the vanity of human life by saying, 'It is all nothing to me now, it is like a dream.' Being of a remarkably active turn, the infirmities of age were peculiarly distressing to him, and he was accustomed to say to his friends, 'Never wish to be old. I am now in the twelfth chapter of Ecclesiastes, and the grasshopper is a burden to me.'"

Literally worn down with the weight of years, he expired at the village of Cirencester, April 1, 1826, having lived twenty years past the allotted age of man. By his own request, his remains were removed to Lechlade and placed in the same tomb where his wife and daughter had been buried but a few years before.

Thus passed from earth, one who had systematized those plans which have done and are destined to do more than all others in making practical the injunction of the wise man, viz : "Train up a child in the way he should go, and when he is old he will not depart from it."

It is said that his known liberality of spirit, to all sects and parties who loved the cause of Christ, gained him many friends among the higher orders of the clergy of the established church, while his exemplary walk and conversation won the hearts of those Christians among dissenters whose peculiar sentiments of church government were very different from his own.

In one particular he was a model, which, if universally followed, would make the whole human family one band of brothers. I allude to the fact that he was a universal peace-maker, and would never suffer any one to be evil spoken of in his presence, without taking the part of the absent one.

Bespecting the person of Mr. Fox, some idea may be formed from the description of one who knew him well, and says that,—"Although of late years, he was regardless of his person, except on particuar occasions, his appearance, when dressed, was very much of the gentleman. He was a little above the middle size, his forehead high, and his eyes, which inclined to blue, remarkably animated when speaking. In earlier life he must have been handsome."

After retiring from business, he used to spend some hours before dinner in the exercise of shooting, which he found quite beneficial to his health. While he lived in London he was much troubled with a nervous headache, and in the morning with great lassitude, but in the country, during the shooting season, every complaint was removed. Having at Lechlade a manor of considerable extent, he was desirous of furnishing his friends, as well as himself with game, which led him to pursue it with more avidity than he otherwise would have done. Indeed as to his own gratification in eating and drinking, particularly the latter, he was a very rare example of abstemiousness, from his childhood.

The following notice of the death of Mr. Fox, may be found in the American Sunday School Magazine for October, 1826.

Death of William Fox, Esq., The Founder of the Sunday-School Society.—On April 1st, 1826, died at Cirencester, in the 91st year of his age, William Fox, Esq., formerly a deacon of the church under the pastoral care of the Rev. Abraham Booth; he had long been in a state of great weakness and infirmity, having realized the striking representation of old age given by the wise man, Ecclesiastes 12: and which was the very frequent subject of his conversation. He continued to the last to take a very lively interest in Sunday School institutions, and would often detail in a very interesting manner, the circumstances connected with the formation of the society, of which he was the founder. A funeral sermon was preached on the occasion of his death, in the Baptist meeting house, Cirencester, from Psalms l. 15, a passage which was selected for the occasion by the deceased.

"And call upon me in the day of trouble, I will deliver thee, and thou shalt glorify me."

In the annual report of the London Sunday School Union, for 1827, his death is also respectfully noticed, and the conviction expressed that the cause of Sunday Schools had lost a devoted friend in William Fox, Esq., the founder of the Sunday School Society.

The following inscription is on the tomb in the burial-ground of the Baptist chapel, at Lechlade, in Gloucestershire, England.

This Stone
Which perpetuates the memory of
MARY EVILL
Who departed this life
April 9th, 1821,
Contains the first records of mortality
ever placed in this ground.
In the same grave also are deposited
the mortal remains of
MARY FOX
mother of the above
who died Feb. 5th, 1823; and of
WILLIAM FOX Esq.
Husband of the aforesaid Mary Fox
of Lechlade House
Who died April 1st 1826

Grave! the Guardian of their dust,
Grave! the Treasury of the Skies
Every atom of thy Trust
Rests in hope again to rise

William Fox had five children, two sons and three daughters. His sons were Jonathan and William His daughters, Sarah, Mary, and Susanna. Jonathan, the eldest, was for many years after his father's death, an eminent merchant in London. He married a Miss Evill, of Bath; they had a number of children, four of whom, one son and three daughters, were living in 1859. One of the daughters is married and resides in London, the other two are unmarried, and reside in Cheshire. The son Henry has long been a ship broker and commission merchant in Liverpool; he was the father of the Australian trade, having been in that business long before Melbourne or the gold diggings were heard of. I received two letters from him in 1859; he had not then retired from business. In one of those letters he says that in the latter part of his father's life, he was accustomed to write a letter containing good advice and instruction, and add ess it to the captain of each vessel despatched by himself, [Henry,] to Australia. The letter was to be opened and read the second Sabbath after leaving Liverpool. It was accompanied by a package of religious tracts, to be distributed at the same time among the passengers and crew. Mr. Henry Fox has one son, Rev. Richard James Lord Fox, and three daughters, each unmarried.

The second son of William Fox, Mr. William Fox, junior, was, long after his father's death, a partner in a banking house in London. He married a Miss Hall, of that city. Being a man of considerable literary attainments, he wrote a number of works on various subjects, which were published. He had four sons living in 1859, two of them in London, and two in the Bath.

The eldest daughter, Sarah, married a gentleman by the name of Samuel Harris, a druggist in London; they had several children, all of whom died in infancy except two, a son and a daughter. After the son, William Tell Harris was married, the whole family removed to America in 1819 or '20 and selected a situation on the west bank of the Ohio river, about twenty-six miles below Cincinnati, at what is now Aurora, in the state of Indiana. Soon after settling here, Mr. Samuel Harris was ordained to the gospel ministry by the proper tribunal of the Baptist church; he, with a number of others, united in forming the first church of any denomination in Aurora. Mr. Harris was the first pastor of the church, he continued to discharge its duties to the end of his life. In the year 1823 he was called upon to part with his beloved companion after a protracted illness. The reader will remember that her mother died the same year; Mrs. Harris was buried in the cemetery on the west side of the town, within a few yards of where the track of the Ohio and Mississippi Railroad now lies. Mr. Harris, in addition to his pastoral labors, was accustomed to preach at many other points in the country around Aurora.

He is particularly remembered for the catholic spirit he always manifested towards ministers of other denominations. In October, 1832, he went to Cincinnati, and stopped at the house of an old friend, William Orange, Esq. That gentleman in a letter to a friend of mine, says, " Mr. Harris died at my house; he came there in good health, with trunks all packed for a long journey through Illinois, with the intention of making a long stay at my brother's, in Alton, but finding the cholera raging in our city, he feared he might take it on his way, and he preferred dying at a friend's house, as he said he always expected he would; he appeared in good spirits up to the time of the attack. I recollect we urged him to play for us on the piano, which he did, and repeated some verses I understood he composed. I have never forgotten the first verse; as near as I can recollect, it is as follows:

"'I have no abiding city here,
To me, this world is dark and drear,
I long to see my father's face,
I long to reach my resting place.'

" This is all I recollect of several verses he repeated to us; he was full of heavenly joy, little thinking he was within a few hours of that eternal home where he longed to be."

Mr. Orange then details the circumstances of his sickness and death, being attacked that night, and expiring the next day about noon, with the half-spoken sentence, "Oh, my dear sir!" upon his lips.

His remains were deposited in the Baptist burying ground on Catharine street, Cincinnati. The following is a part of the inscription on his tomb—"To Samuel Harris, late Pastor of the Baptist church in Aurora, [Ind.] who died of Asiatic cholera Oct. 19, 1832, in the 65th year of his age." Mr. Harris was a fine scholar, familiar with a number of languages, easy in his manners, and was much beloved and respected in all the relations of life.

A short time before the death of Mrs. Harris, their only daughter married Mr. S. Lawford, a woollen manufacturer of Leeds, England. After crossing the Atlantic ocean five times, Mrs. Lawford died at Aurora in the summer of 1849. She was buried near her mother. William T. Harris, the only son of the Rev. Samuel Harris, continues to reside in Aurora (1862.) He had two children, a son and a daughter—the son died in infancy; the daughter is married, and resides in a western city.

The second daughter of Mr. Fox, Mary, married Mr. William Evill. They had but one child, a daughter, who bore her mother's name. She was born in the year 1795. Being a delicate child from infancy, she required much care and attention from her mother. In the year 1804, when little Mary was in her ninth year, she was left with her grandparents at Lechlade, so that her mother was deprived of seeing her for several months. During that time she employed some leisure hours in writing out all the particulars she could remember and collect of Mary's past life. This little biography abounds with expressions of anxiety she felt for the spiritual welfare of her child. In a little introductory address she informs Mary that it is for her present perusal, signifies her intention to continue the record, and expresses the hope that she may furnish something more worthy to be written before it is closed, and gives her such advice as every parent should who is training a soul for immortality.

Soon after receiving this little memoir, Mary wrote to her mother proposing an interchange of their thoughts by writing, and was responded to by the mother, who usually made it convenient to have an epistle for her perusal on Sabbath mornings, when she was unable to attend public worship.

The mother's faithfulness was blessed in leading the child to the Saviour; she died before she was fifteen years of age, on the 30th of September, 1810. In the first note to her mother she enclosed an epitaph for herself, which she says was written thinking that by looking at it sometimes it might awaken serious reflections. It is engraved on her tombstone beneath the date of her birth and death, and reads as follows—

"In the early part of her life she suffered much from bodily weakness; murmured often; was very impatient and fretful; fearful of offending her God—yet not obeying, loving or serving him as she ought; longing to know more of him, but seeking him seldom. She lived with the earnest wish, yet faint hope of one day joining the happy and glorious throng above.—Amen."

Her mother, as has already been stated, died in 1821; her grandfather in 1826; and in 1838 all the papers and letters between her mother and herself were collected, arranged, and published for circulation among the friends and relations of the family, under the title of "Memoir of Mary Evill, grand-daughter of the late William Fox, Esq., of Lechlade." The little volume contains one hundred and eighty-one pages, and with a little revision would make an excellent Sunday School book.

Susanna, the third and youngest daughter of Mr. Fox, was never married.

Mr. Fox was personally acquainted and on terms of intimacy with Jonas Hanway, Granville Sharpe, and John Howard, Esqs., whose well known philanthropy would naturally produce this association of kindred spirits. Although it does not properly belong to this work, I hope the reader will pardon me for giving a brief sketch of the three last named gentlemen—their lives being a part of the history of Sunday Schools.

Jonas Hanway was born in 1712 at Portsmouth, England. At an early age he was bound apprentice to a merchant in Lisbon, Portugal, after which he became connected with a commercial house in St. Petersburgh, Russia, which led him to visit Persia.

On leaving Russia he settled in London, and in 1753 published an account of his travels in two volumes—also in four. He was a prolific author, considering that he was an active and enterprising merchant—his writings amounted to seventy volumes.

It is mentioned of him as a curiosity, that he was the first man ever known to carry a raised umbrella in the streets of London—so recently have those necessary articles come into use. Mr. Hanway will be longest remembered by his works of charity, among which may be mentioned his assistance in organizing and supporting the Mariners' Society and the Magdalene Society. He also exerted himself to ameliorate the condition of the London chimney-sweeps, besides being engaged in many other benevolent enterprises. We should naturally expect such a man to favor the establishment of Sunday Schools by supporting a Society to make them general. His well known benevolence caused him to be appointed a Commissioner of the Navy by the British Government, and when he retired his salary was continued. He died in 1789, and a monument was erected to his memory in Westminster Abbey.

Granville Sharpe was born at Durham, England, in 1724. It was once claimed by British subjects in the colonies of England, that they had a right to take their negro slaves into England when there on visits of business or pleasure—just as the slaveholders of our southern States have claimed the same privilege when visiting our free States. Through the influence of Mr. Sharpe, the British Government was induced to recognize the freedom of every human being as soon as he or she set their feet on English soil. He was founder of the colony of Sierra Leone, South Africa—also of the Abolition Society of England, and was quite active in the formation of the British and Foreign Bible Society.

Mr. Sharpe was a warm and consistent friend of Sabbath Schools from the commencement. He died July 6, 1813, aged seventy-nine.

John Howard was born at Hackney, England, in 1726. Having been taken prisoner by a French pirate vessel in early life, and his having suffered severely during that imprisonment, is said to have been partly the cause of his turning his attention to the treatment of prisoners generally. But it was not until he was appointed to the office of sheriff in one of the counties of England that he determined to devote his life to benevolent labors. His life was yielded a sacrifice to the cause in which he was engaged. Having gone to Turkey to ascertain the nature of the plague, with a view of discovering some means of curing it, he died of that epidemic at Cherson, Jan. 20, 1790, aged sixty-four.

A conotaph has been erected to his memory in St. Paul's Cathedral, London. But the numerous Howard Associations for the relief of suffering humanity, in the large cities of our own and other lands, are the most appropriate monuments to his memory and virtues.

CHAPTER XV.

In the first chapter, I alluded to the fact of Sunday Schools having been established in the latter part of the sixteenth century, in the city of Milan, Lombardy, by Charles Borromeo, Archbishop of Milan. In the American Sunday School Magazine for January, 1825, may be found a description of these schools by the Rev. Daniel Wilson, a distinguished clergyman of London, under the title of "Letters from an absent brother." The letter containing the description was dated

MILAN, Sept. 14, 1823.

"After English service, we went to see the catechising. This was founded by Borromeo, in the sixteenth century, and is peculiar to Milan. The children meet in classes of ten or twenty, drawn up between the pillars of the vast Cathedral, and separated from each other by curtains, the boys on one side, and the girls on the other. In all the churches of the city there are classes also. Many grown people are mingled with the children. A priest sat in the midst of each class, and seemed to be familiarly explaining the Christian religion. The sight was quite interesting. Tables for learning to write were placed in the different recesses. The children were exceedingly attentive. At the door of each school the words 'Pax Vobis,' 'Peace be unto you,' were inscribed on boards. Each scholar had a small pulpit, with a green cloth in front, bearing the Borromean motto 'Humilitas.' "

The writer asks what can be more excellent than all this, and then proceeds :—" But mark the corruption of Popery, these poor children are all made members of a fraternity, and purchase indulgences for their sins by coming to school. A brief of the Pope, dated 1609, affords a perpetual indulgence to the children in a sort of running lease of six thousand years, eight thousand years, &c., and these indulgences are applicable to the recovery of souls out of purgatory. Then the prayers before school are full of error and idolatry. All this I saw with my own eyes, and heard with my own ears, for I was curious to understand the bearings of these celebrated schools. Thus is the infant mind fettered. Still I do not doubt that much good may be done on the whole ; the [Roman] Catholic catechisms contain admirable instruction, and much evangelical matter, though mixed up with folly and superstition."

In another part of his letter, Mr. Wilson says:—"May I not add that some of the superstitious usages now attached to these schools, may have grown up since the time of Borromeo. Certainly, the indulgences I saw there were of the date of 1609, five-and-twenty years after his death."

In a work entitled a "Classical Tour through Italy," which was republished in this country in 1814, the same schools are thus alluded to:—"In the diocese of Milan, or in that vast tract of country included between the Alps and the Appenines, and subject to the archiepiscopal see of Milan, in every parochial church, the bells toll at two in the afternoon of every Sabbath in the year, and all the youth of the parish assemble in the church; the girls are placed on one side, the boys on the other, they are then divided into classes according to their ages and progress, and instructed either by the clergy attached to the church, or by pious persons who voluntarily devote their time to this most useful employment; while the pastor himself goes from class to class, examines sometimes one, sometimes another, and closes the whole at four by a catechistical discourse."

We can see how the importance of a system for collecting the children on the Sabbath to communicate religious instruction to them has been pressing upon the minds of Christians for centuries. And that this was the largest enterprise in that direction of which we have any knowledge previous to 1781—2. This system never could have become general, for it was utterly unsuited to the wants of England, America, or any other than a Catholic country.

I will now endeavor to give the reader a condensed view of Sabbath Schools to the end of the lives of the founders of the present system. In order to do this, it will be necessary to recapitulate. The first schools were established by Mr. Raikes, in 1781—2. The first society by Mr. Fox, Sept. 7, 1785. The Edinburgh Gratis Sabbath School Society, March, 1797. The London Sunday School Union, July 13, 1803. The Sunday School Society for Ireland, November, 1809. The Nottingham and Hampshire Sunday School Union, in 1810, besides many others, such as the London Hibernian Society, the Bristol Adult School Society, and the Gainsborough Adult Sunday School Society.

While these societies were being organized in Great Britain, efforts were constantly made by them to spread the good work to other countries, and it soon became a settled principle, that whenever a missionary started for a foreign land, the Sabbath School must be introduced and relied on as one of the most efficient implements of aggressive warfare against the strongholds of ignorance, superstition, and vice. All sectarianism seemed to vanish, ministers and laymen of all denominations labored with a zeal worthy of the cause in which they were engaged, the main object being to give the word of life to all the world, without regard to the effect it would have on this or that denomination. The limits of this work will not admit of detail. I will briefly state that in EUROPE, besides being established in England, Ireland, Scotland, and Wales, schools were established in many parts of France, chiefly in the south. They were also established in Holland and Germany. In Spain, at Giberaltar, on the island of Malta, and in Greece. In ASIA, they had been established in India, at Calcutta, Madras, Bombay, Bengalove, Bellary, Chinsurah, Chittagong, Veperey, and Vizagapatam. In Ceylon, the first school established on this island was at Calumbo, June 4, 1815, by the Rev. W. M. Harvard. They were also about this time, established in New South Wales.

In the British penal colony of Van Dieman's land, they were organized. At Kangaroo Point, Hobart's Town, and some other places. In the South sea Islands at Huahine and Moimili. Mr. Charles Barff, formerly a Sunday School teacher in London, writing to the Sunday School Union from Huahine, says :— "We are happy to inform you that we have, in addi tion to day schools, a Sunday School at Huahine. It is confined exclusively to children ; the number in the school is two hundred and thirty boys, and one hundred and twenty girls. The reason why the boys are more numerous than the girls, is the female children were more frequently murdered than were male children, in their horrid custom of infanticide; the males were saved for purposes of war. All such horrid customs have long since fallen with their idolatry, we hope never to rise again. The children are instructed by pious native teachers, six females, and six males, besides the superintendent."

In another letter Mr. Barff mentions the fact of their having two kings with their wives engaged as teachers in the Sunday Schools, and they esteem their offices in the schools more highly than in the government.

In Western Africa, "Sunday Schools had been established by the church and Methodist Missionary Society, but on account of the deaths of so many of the missionaries, they have been exposed to considerable fluctuations."

In South Africa, Sunday Schools have been established at Cape Town, also at several Missionary Stations in the interior. A Sunday School Union had been established for the district of Albany. The Union contains three hundred children, of whom one hundred and thirty are Hottentots and slaves.

"In the Mauritius, or Isle of France, Mr. Le Brun established a Sunday School."

"In Madagascar the children under tuition are about twelve hundred. The king takes a lively interest in the schools. On the Sabbath day, the children are catechised from six to eight in the morning, both in English and Malagash. At half past one, they are questioned on general subjects, and the Scriptures are read by them and translated into their own language ; at half past four they meet again to sing a few hymns in English and Malagash. Several catechisms, and elementary books, and a small collection of hymns, have been prepared."

I have been unable to be very accurate in dates, but what I have given with regard to Madagascar, and all other points on the last few pages, occurred previous to 1825.

"In the West Indies, Sabbath Schools were established in various places, but it is said the Island of Antigua has been most successful ; schools were established there in 1810 by the Missionaries of the established Church of England, the Wesleyan Missionaries and the Moravians. On the island of Barbadoes schools were in in operation previous to the insurrection in 1816 ; what a marked difference was manifested between those slaves that had received religious instruction, and those who had not ; the former being peaceful and orderly ; the latter, turbulent and brutal."

"On the Island of Hayti, St. Domingo, Sabbath Schools have bnen established among the emigrants from the United States of America. A society was organized at Port au Platte, called the Haytian Sunday School Union. The Wesleyan Missionaries were particularly active in forming schools in the Bermudas, the Bahama Islands, the Caribbee Islands, in Jamaica, and in Demerara."

"In South America, they were early established at Buenos Ayres. In North America, on Newfoundland, Sabbath Schools were early formed in many of the settlements with encouraging success."

Nova Scotia. Here about one thousand scholars are taught in the different Sabbath Schools by nearly fifty teachers. Schools are also in operation in New Brunswick, Cape Breton, and Prince Edwards Island.

A letter written in 1858, from a gentleman by the name of Moore, on Prince Edwards Island, to a friend in England, speaking of the powerful influence of Sunday Schools, and of the great work of the Sunday School Society in organizing a system to spread them throughout the world, says,—"Myself and family will ever revere the name of Fox, the founder of the Sunday School Society, as it was through the instrumentality of those schools that myself, wife, and six children were brought to a knowledge of the truth as it is in Jesus."

The letter does not say whether they came under the influence of the schools before leaving England, or after their home was on the Island. They were Wesleyan Methodists.

In Canada, although the population is scattered, Sabbath Schools were early appreciated. In 1824, the legislature of Upper Canada appropriated one hundred and fifty pounds, (seven hundred and fifty dollars,) to promote these institutions generally, without any distinction of name or party. Previous to that time, they had a general Sunday School Union for the whole of Canada, besides minor Unions at York and Niagara.

CHAPTER XVI.

It is somewhat difficult to determine the exact time or place of establishing the first Sunday Schools in this country, or even to notice all the claims to that distinguished honor, for they (the claims) spring up all along from Maine, or at least from Massachusetts to Georgia. In the introductory chapter I briefly noticed the claims of Plymouth, Mass., Savannah, Ga., Bethlehem, Conn., and Ephrata, Pa., previous to 1781—2.

Each of these places supposed theirs were the first Sunday Schools in America, and some of them thought they were the first in the world.

After the organization of Sunday Schools in England by Mr. Raikes in 1781—2, the first we know of them in this country is from Gorrie's History of the Methodist Episcopal Church. He says that as early as 1784, " the Methodist ministers were required by the Discipline, whenever there were ten children whose parents were members, to meet them at least an hour every week for purposes of religious instruction."

In Strickland's Life of Asbury, Chapter XI., the following sentence may be found, in speaking of Bishop Asbury's connection with Sunday Schools. He says—" In 1786, five years before any other person moved in this matter, he organized his schools in Hanover county, Va." Gorrie says, " As early as 1786 Sunday Schools were established in the Methodist Episcopal Church in the United States, through the agency of Bishop Asbury, who being in constant communication with Mr. Wesley by correspondence, learned from the latter the fact of their establishment in England."

Charleston, S. C., seems entitled to peculiar honor with regard to the introduction of Sunday Schools into this country. Dr. McClintock, in the Methodist Quarterly Review for 1859, is disposed to give them full credit for their arduous, self-denying, and *characteristic* labors in behalf of down-trodden humanity. He says—" In 1787 George Daughaday, a Methodist preacher in Charleston, S. C., was drenched with water pumped from a public cistern, ' for the crime of conducting a Sunday School for the benefit of the African children of that vicinity.' "

Dr. McClintock also says that " The Minutes of 1790 contain the first church legislation on the subject known, perhaps either in Europe or America." According to Mr. Gorrie, who alludes to the same legislation which was made a part of the Discipline, " the ministers and preachers were required to establish Sunday Schools in or near the places of worship, for the benefit of white and black children, and to appoint suitable persons to teach gratis all who would attend, and who had a capacity to learn." These early efforts seem not to have been attended with very great success.

The first schools that after being planted really took root and grew to a flourishing condition, were those organized and fostered by "The First-day or Sunday School Society of Philadelphia." The first meeting preparatory to organizing such a society, was held in the city of Philadelphia, Dec. 19, 1790, and was attended by some of the most distinguished citizens of the place. Among these may be mentioned the Right Rev. William White, D. D., Bishop of Pennsylvania, who was consecrated to the Episcopal office Feb. 4, 1787, Dr. Benjamin Rush, whose reputation as a physician is world-wide, Dr. William Currie, Mr. Thomas Mendenhall, Mr. Peter Thompson, Jun., Mr. Matthew Carey, Mr. Thomas P. Cope, Captain Nathaniel Falconer, Mr. Joseph Sharpless, Robert Ralston, Paul Beck, Jun., William Raule, Thomas Armat, and others.

On the 26th day of the same month, another meeting was held, and a constitution for the society adopted, On the 11th of January, 1791, the officers were elected and the society organized. From some cause unexplained, no school was formed until March following. The preamble to the constitution states the object of the society in the following language—

"Whereas the good education of youth is of the first importance to society, and numbers of children, the offspring of indigent parents, have not proper opportunities of instruction previous to their being apprenticed to trades; And whereas among the youth of every large city various instances occur of the first day of the week, called Sunday, a day which ought to be devoted to religious improvement, being employed to the worst of purposes, the depravity of morals and manners—it is therefore the opinion of sundry persons that the establishment of First day or Sunday Schools in this city would be of essential advantage to the rising generation—and for effecting that benevolent purpose, they have formed themselves into a society, by the name of the Society for the institution and support of First day or Sunday Schools in the city of Philadelphia, and the districts of Southwark and the Northern Liberties."

Although it is not stated that the men who projected this institution were acquainted with what had been done in England, it is presumed they were, from the similarity of their plans in many respects, and that they both employed paid teachers.

One Quaker, Samuel Hoare, was present and took part in the organization of the first society in England. The name of this society would seem to indicate that there was a Quaker influence in its organization.

In December, 1791, the Board of Officers presented a memorial to the Legislature of Pennsylvania, urging the establishment of free schools, which the constitution of that state empowered them to do. At that time the society had three schools containing near two hundred pupils. Early in 1792 the board appropriated ten pounds, (fifty dollars,) to be laid out in small moral books to be lent to the scholars, or given as premiums to the most deserving. In July, 1793 the society agreed that the instructions given in their schools should be confined to writing and reading from the Bible. For such pupils as had not learned to read, spelling books and primers might be used. It appears from this rule, that it was not a primary object of the society to disseminate religious instruction; the principal aim being to improve the pupils in the common rudiments of reading, writing, and decency of behavior. These, of themselves, were of great importance, but many favorable opportunities to impress the minds of the young with religious truths, must have been lost. The city was visited by the yellow fever in 1793; the schools were suspended, and several of the society fell victims to that desease. It was during the prevalence of that epidemic that Dr. Rush, one of the founders of the society, became famous by his great skill, and almost superhuman exertions to render medical assistance to all classes, making no distinction between rich and poor.

The schools were resumed the following winter. From the beginning in March, 1791, to Jan., 1795, there had been admitted into the three schools, nine hundred and fifty-four pupils, one hundred and eighty of whom remained under instruction at that time. The receipts of the society during that time amounted to seven hundred and ten pounds, fourteen shillings, and a half-penny ; or a little over four thousand and fifty dollars, and the expenses for teachers' salaries, filling and delivering notices to the members to attend the meetings, with other incidental expenses, amounted to six hundred and fifty-three pounds, three shillings and five pence ; or about three thousand two hundred and sixty-five dollars, leaving a balance of about seven hundred and eighty-five dollars. The board of visitors then stated that the utility and success which have attended this mode of education, have been equal to the expectations of the society. They say, "there are, at present, many instances among the males and females, of pupils, who, without any other opportunity of acquiring the benefits of a school, than that afforded by this society, are now capable of reading and spelling with correctness and propriety, and of writing an easy, fair, and legible hand. Besides which, they have been, in a great measure, prevented from misspending their time on Sunday, and from acquiring a habit of idleness, which often proves a source of public, as well as private misfortune."

In 1797, the society succeeded in procuring an act of incorporation from the proper authorities, for which they had applied three years before.

Their corporate character is indicated in their legal proceedings by a plain, neat seal, with the following motto,—"Licet Sabbatis Benefacere, Incorporated 1797." And in a circle on the border are the words, —"First Day, or Sunday School Society of Philadelphia." From March, 1791, to January, 1800, the sum of three thousand nine hundred and sixty-eight dollars had been received, and nearly that sum expended in the support of the schools. During that period two thousand one hundred and twenty-seven scholars had been admitted into the schools, and the attendance was about one hundred and eighty at a time. The average expense for nine years was four hundred and three dollars, being about two dollars and twenty-five cents per annum for each scholar; much more than the expenses of the present plan of Sunday Schools, and forty cents more than the schools on the Lancasterian plan, where they were taught five days in the week.

The following extract from "Raikes and his Sunday Schools," will explain the system of teaching alluded to above, and give you some information of the man who originated it.

"In the year 1839, Joseph Lancaster, of whom we have already spoken as a friend of Robert Raikes, was suddenly removed from earth, aged sixty-eight years. He was well known as the originator of a new system of education, which, for many years bore his name, 'The Lancasterian system;' the great popularity of which, was the employment of advanced pupils to instruct the class next below themselves; and these again to instruct others of a still lower grade; and so on through the whole school, each grade in proficiency becoming the teachers of a lower class. For many years he was actively engaged in England, in the work of lecturing, and planting the schools in which he took so intense an interest. In an interview with George III., he received that sovereign's declaration,—'I hope the time will come when every poor child in my dominions will be able to read the Bible.' As might have been expected, wherever Lancaster went, the novelty of his project drew around him the curious and the benevolent; including those possessed of rank and wealth, as well as very many who sympathized in all such efforts to benefit mankind. The British and foreign schools in the Borough Road, London, originated in his zeal. But, though he was greatly applauded, Lancaster was the subject of poverty, often, indeed, extreme. Hoping to avoid its evils, he came to this country, where he expected, from the general love to the cause of education, to obtain a better support. Here, however, he found his improvements were already in use, and his circumstances were but little improved. He traveled very extensively through our country ; lectured three times before Congress, and enjoyed the friendship of many of the best men in the land. But poverty, and his utter ignorance of economy, still depressed him, and the independence for which he toiled, never came. He died in New York, from an injury occasioned by being run over in the street by an omnibus. Joseph Lancaster was attached to the Society of Friends."

We will now finish our sketch of the First Day or Sunday School Society. In 1810 the board published a summary account of their proceedings during the preceding nineteen years ; but did not state the number of scholars admitted since 1800. The total receipts up to July 1810, amounted to seven thousand six hundred and thirty-nine dollars and sixty-three cents. From 1810 to 1815–16, when Sabbath Schools were established by gratuitous teachers, this society continued their schools much in the same way as in former years.

The venerable Bishop White has been president of this society more than thirty-three years, that is from its commencement; a few of its founders and early patrons remain, but many have fallen asleep. The account I give of this society was taken from an article in the October number of the American Sunday School Magazine for 1824. From "Raikes and his friends," I learn that the society was in existence as late as 1859, with an income of about three thousand dollars from accumulated funds. The income was still appropriated to the support of Sunday Schools. Don't let the society die, friends, but keep it, and let Jan. 11, 1791, be remembered as the day on which the first Sunday School Society was organized in America.

It is said that in the same year, [1791] Mr. Collier, a Baptist student in Brown University, opened a Sunday School in Pawtucket, Rhode Island; he was assisted by Mr. Samuel Slater, who first introduced machinery for the manufacture of cotton, into this country.

The first Sunday School in the state of New York, was organized in the year 1792, at Stockbridge, in the house of an Indian woman; a sister of the Rev. Samson Occum. Mr. Occum was a distinguished Indian preacher. The school was not commenced until a few months after his death.

CHAPTER XVII.

In Passaic county, New Jersey, a cotton manufacturing company, in 1794, employed a teacher to instruct gratuitously on the Sabbath, the children employed in the factory. That is thought to have been the first Sabbath School in New Jersey.

The Rev. S. Wilmer commenced a Sabbath School, in 1806, at Kent, Maryland, which is believed to have been the first in that State. In 1809, according to Lloyd, in his "Life of Raikes," a society was formed in Pittsburg, Pennsylvania, then only a village. The object of which society was :—"The suppression of vice, reformation of manners, and the propagation of useful knowledge." This led to the adoption of measures for instructing and improving the moral condition of the poorer classes of the community. A benevolent gentleman suggested the advantages of a school for religious instruction on the Sabbath. Such a school was accordingly formed August 22, 1809, of which public notice had previously been given, soliciting the attendance of scholars and the co-operation of the citizens.

This excited a considerable degree of interest, and

the school was opened on the first Sabbath in September, and attended by two hundred and forty scholars, children and adults. It is said the school was organized without a knowledge of the system pursued in Europe, and in its main features was similar to those established on a more liberal plan. Our authority does not state whether teachers were paid or not.

For the purpose of giving my authority, I shall be under the necessity of coming down nearer to the present date than I desired, although the events treated of occurred prior to 1826.

A Sabbath school celebration was held at Beverly, Massachusetts, on the fifth of September, 1860. A historical address was delivered on the occasion by the Rev. A. B. Rich, of that place. In his address, Mr. Rich stated that in the summer of 1809, two young ladies, Miss Hannah Hill and Miss Joanna B. Prince, organized a Sabbath School in that town, in consequence of hearing of the success of Raikes' schools in England.

They were assisted and encouraged by two other devoted Christian women, one of them being blind, the other, Mrs. Meservey, was a member of the Methodist church. Miss Hill never married; she died in Beverly, March 16, 1838. Miss Prince was married to Ebenezer Everett, and removed to Brunswick, Maine, in 1819. She died Sept. 5, 1859, having served half a century as a Sabbath school teacher.

It is believed that the first suggestions of Sabbath Schools in this country on the present plan of gratuitous teachers, was made by the Rev. Robert May, a missionary from London. Mr. May was the son of a common mariner at Woodbridge, England, and when a very ragged little boy was induced to enter a Sunday School, where he learned to love the Saviour, and was admitted to the Independent or Congregational church in that town, and not long after began to prepare for the ministry, with a view to becoming a missionary in foreign lands. In a letter to the Evangelical Society of Philadelphia in the summer of 1811, he proposed the establishment of Sunday Schools, furnished specimens of the tickets then used, and explained the mode of operation. An association was formed, a school established Oct. 20, 1811, which was conducted under the personal direction of Mr. May himself, until his return to Europe in 1812.

This account is taken from Lloyd's life of Raikes, but the Rev. Joseph Belcher, author of "Raikes, his Sunday Schools and his Friends," thinks it must have been a year earlier, and that the schools were opened in Philadelphia in 1810. Dr. Belcher says that Mr. May sailed for India in the early part of 1811. The same author says that, "In India he superintended schools containing three thousand children, and was about to add two thousand five hundred to their number, when, in 1818, death suddenly terminated his continuance on earth."

It is said the first Sunday School in Delaware was commenced at Wilmington, in 1814, and in the same year the first one on the improved plan was organized in the Baptist church, Chanes street, Boston, as the result of a visit to New York by the wife of the pastor, Rev. Dr. Sharpe.

In June, 1814, Mrs. Isabella Graham and her daughter, Mrs. Bethune, wife of Davie Bethune, organized a Sunday chool in the city of New York. By this time a general interest began to be felt in the cause of Sunday Schools in this country. Mrs. Graham died July 27, 1814, but a little over a month from the organization of the first school. Her son-in-law, Davie Bethune, was a Scotchman by birth ; he became a wealthy merchant in New York.

He was a devoted Christian, and a liberal supporter of every benevolent enterprise. In a letter to Stephen Prust, of Bristol, England, dated July 13, 1814, Mr. Bethune, after thanking Mr. Brust for a copy of Dr. Pole's "History of Adult Schools," says :—"Mrs. Bethune, and about twenty other ladies, have petitioned the corporation of the city to grant them the use of a building erected for a house of industry. Mrs. B. is of opinion an Adult School may very properly be attached to such an institution." A letter from the same to the same, June 10, 1815, contained the following passage :—"It will be gratifying to you to learn, that your transmission of the Report of the Adult Schools has been the means of awakening great interest in this object *here*, and in Philadelphia. I forward you an extract of a letter I received from a pious young lady in Philadelphia, to whom I mentioned the Adult Schools when there, in January last. The little school began by Mrs. B. on her reading Dr. Pole's report, has succeeded astonishingly. She and my two daughters, assisted by a female friend, teach it on Sunday mornings. It consists of between eighty and ninety; and the Bible class, now all able to read, is forty-seven! Schools for the education of poor children are rapidly increasing in this country."

The following is an extract from the letter of Miss S. Whitehead, of Philadelphia, referred to by Mr. Bethune. She says :—"I had several extracts from Dr. Pole's work inserted in the 'Religious Remembrancer,' a weekly paper of our city, and the subject excited universal attention. The Freemasons have taken it up, and at a general meeting, it was proposed and carried unanimously, that several schools should be established, and held in the Grand Lodge, Chestnut street! There is no doubt that all the different Lodges belonging to the fraternity will take up this subject, and it will *extend over the whole Union;* one of the officers gave me this information."

The Masons did engage in the cause, but not to 'extend over the whole Union.' What a pity! They could not have done for humanity a more benevolent act, or secured for themselves more lasting honor. Miss Whitehead continues :—" Mr. Thomas Bradford commenced a school in the jail last Sabbath day. Several pious female friends of mine propose shortly to commence one in the west end of the city, and thus you see 'how great a matter a little fire kindleth.' O, come let us sing praises to the Lord. O, my soul, and all that is within me, praise His holy name!

" I never undertook anything that afforded me such *heartfelt-joy*; our precious little establishment goes on delightfully. The first member was a pious soul, fifty years of age; she comes with her spectacles on, and seems as if she would devour the book. She never fails giving us a blessing, and assures us she has *long been praying* that the Lord would open some way that she might learn to read the Bible; she looks at your little book with delight, and often says,—' O, this blessed book, I know I shall learn to read in this book.' I feel as if her prayers were as good as a host. We have eleven scholars, two added mostly of an [nearly every] evening, and after the first lesson they advance wonderfully. O what encouragement for prayers is this. Open wide thy mouth, and I will fill it, saith the Lord. Great exertions have been made for the relief of the body, but O, the soul that never dies, that anything should be done for that is transporting. That the soul be without knowledge is not good. Our city exhibits improvement in morality and religion, the cause of temperance is advancing, our churches are better attended and vital piety is progressing."

It may not be amiss to give some extracts from a letter written by Mrs. Bethune, Jan. 24, 1816, to her friends in Bristol, England. "I cannot resist the desire I feel to employ my pen in thanking you for your presents to myself and children, of so many interesting publications from which I trust we have derived both profit and pleasure. I believe I cannot express my gratitude in a manner better suited to your liberal soul, than by giving you an account of a meeting held this day in this city. Mr. Bethune published one of your letters in one of our daily papers. I lent the different publications relative to Sunday Schools, to a number of our friends, and was in hopes the gentlemen would have come forward in the business, but after waiting a number of weeks, I conversed with several of my own sex, who expressed a wish to unite with me in a Female Sunday School Union. Accordingly we called a meeting of the female members of all denominations, who met this day in the lecture room of one of our churches. Although the notice was not as general as intended, several hundred were present. Dr. Romeyn opened the meeting with a very appropriate prayer. When he withdrew, the ladies were pleased to call me to the chair. I addressed the company in a few words, stating for what purpose their attendance was requested ; the great need of such an institution in a city where numbers of one sex were training for the gallows and states prison, and of the other for prostitution. Likewise the great want of religious instruction in our small schools. The parents of children attending such, not having time to teach them, would, probably, gladly avail themselves of Sunday Schools, if within their reach. I said, in order to stimulate them to so good a work, I would read them several extracts from British publications, which would show them how much the Lord blessed such institutions in the OLD WORLD ; and concluded by hoping that he would extend his blessings to his hand-maidens, in their attempts to train up a seed to serve him in the NEW WORLD.

"'The following extracts were then read : 'First part of the report of the London Sunday School Union. The second report of the Hibernian Sunday School Society. Two letters from the Rev. Mr. Charles, of Bala, to the London society. Mr. P's two letters to D. B. The swearing father reproved by his child, a Sunday School scholar ; and concluded with the Salopian Adult Scholars' Address, from the Teacher's Magazine.' I may venture to affirm *there was not a dry eye in the room*, and tears flowed copiously down the cheeks of many. After some conversation I called upon the ladies of different denominations, who were willing to collect scholars and subscriptions, to come forward, which they did, from all except one, which I regret to say, we had neglected to notify, the Moravians.

" A committee, consisting of one or two from each denomination, was appointed to form a constitution, and general rules for the Union and schools under their care, to be laid before the society at a meeting this day week. The committee will meet at my house two days hence. I trust, with the blessing of the Lord, we shall see Sabbath Schools in every part of the city in a few weeks. I read the rules of the Bristol Sunday School, which I think we shall adopt, with a very few alterations. I opened a school for ADULT BLACKS last Sunday moring, and I shall send you copies of our rules, reports, &c., as soon as published, Thus may those united in Christ, although separated by the Atlantic, provoke each other to good works, until we meet around the throne to join the spirits of the just made perfect. Hallelujah, glory be to that God who works all our works in us.

" Be so good as to communicate the contents of this letter to our friends, Mr. B.'s family, and should you think that it would give pleasure to the friends of Sunday Schools, to hear that their translantic brethren are following their good example, I have only to request that you will withhold my name. Sincerely wishing you success in your works of faith and labor of love,

I am yours, &c.

J. B."

The following is from Davie Bethune to his friend, Mr. Prust, of Bristol, England:

NEW YORK, Feb. 4, 1816.

I have had little to communicate to you in return for all the valuable information you were so kind as to send me by Captain C———, on subjects of religious interest, or moral improvement. One effect of our zeal, however, will, I doubt not, prove a sufficient reward for your labor of love. *This city is in a stir throughout*; a strong interest awakened, and great exertions commenced for the instruction on Sabbath days of *children and adults.* Mrs. Bethune has written to you an account of the first meeting of the ladies; on that day week the second meeting was held, and so great was the crowd of ladies pressing forward, that the company had to adjourn from a lecture room to a church. Next Sabbath, I believe, was appointed for the commencement of the work of teaching; the zeal of three of the congregations led them to begin this day. Mrs. B. visited these three schools, which, with a school of BLACK ADULTS taught by my family, made up one hundred and thirty-six scholars. I presume the number of children next Lord's-day, will amount to one thousand in all the schools. I had forgot to mention that at the second meeting of the ladies, a society was formed, and a constitution drawn up, following very closely the plan which you had sent us.

Mrs. B. was elected first directress, and a pious friend of hers, Mrs. M., second directress, with a view to aid the superintendents and teachers of the several schools, and to take a general charge of the concerns of the institution. The constitution will soon be published, and we shall send you a copy of it. I believe the gentlemen are mustering their numbers to follow the example of the ladies, and to take charge of the adults and children of their own sex.

The same writer under date of Febuary 10, 1816, says,—

" The gentlemen of this city are busily engaged, and a general meeting called on Monday next, for the organization of a society for the instruction of children and adults."

In July, 1816, the total number of scholars admitted by the New York Female Sunday School Union, was three thousand one hundred and thirty-six, and two hundred and fifty teachers. By the Male Sunday

School Union, two thousand five hundred scholars, and two hundred and fifty teachers.

The first annual report of these two societies showed that five thousand had been admitted up to that time.

From the beginning until 1822, about six hundred of the teachers and pupils had been received as members of the different churches, from the New York Sunday Schools, and about thirty had entered upon a course of preparation for the ministry.

We have been noticing societies and the different organizations for spreading schools, but we have not yet done with individual schools.

In the fall of 1815, at the suggestion of Mrs. Ann Rhees, the first Sabbath School of the First Baptist Church of Philadelphia, was opened. When the pastor of the church, Dr. Holcombe, was consulted about it, he seemed to have but little faith in the project, but smiling, replied, "Well, my sisters, you can but try it; blossoms are sweet and beautiful, even if they produce no fruit."

The first Episcopal Sunday School in the United States, is said to have been organized in connection with St. Paul's Church, Philadelphia, in the latter part of 1816.

Although among the earliest efforts for Sunday Schools in this country, Virginia has claims, as we have already shown in the case of Bishop Asbury, but we have no account of any great prosperity attending them until 1816, when a school was organized in Lynchburg. "The Virginian," of that place, in 1849, after having detailed the circumstances of its organization, says,—

"In a very short time two hundred scholars of both sexes were collected, many of whom had no other opportunity of acquiring the slightest education. It is not possible to say what amount of good may have been done by a single year's existence of the school. We confine ourselves to two cases which have been brought to our notice. Among the first scholars who attended, was a slim, spare youth, who manifested a capacity and desire for improvement. That youth grew up, removed to the West, studied law, and has long been known to the nation as the Honorable William Allen, late Senator of the United States from Ohio. In the second year of the school there was entered as a scholar, a younger boy of prepossessing appearance and deportment. He was the son of one of the founders of the school, and is now the Honorable Isaac P. Walker, Senator in Congress, from the State of Wisconsin."

I find another statement in "Raikes and his Sunday Schools," that on the second Sabbath in April, 1816, a Sabbath School was organized in the Baptist church called Ground Squirrel in Hanover Co., Virginia. Its organization was effected by a young man of the name of Jesse Snead, who was teaching a school on the farm upon which Patrick Henry was born and brought up. Mr. Snead, then twenty-two years of age, having previously met with a tract detailing the origin of a Sunday School in London on Raikes's plan, felt that if it could be brought into operation there, it would assist many to begin an education who would not otherwise enjoy that privilege. He first secured the co-operation of Charles P. Goodall, Captain of a military company. At the April training of the company, Captain Goodall formed the men in a hollow square, and told them what had been done in England for the Sabbath School cause, and invited those friendly to the object to meet at the Ground Squirrel meeting-house, to organize a Sunday School free of charge. Funds were there subscribed for the purchase of books, and on the next Sabbath the school went into operation. From this point it is said the good work was much extended. Mr. Snead was but a few years ago the senior deacon in the Second Baptist church, in Richmond.

CHAPTER XVIII.

Dr. Fowler in his "American Pulpit" says that the Rev. now Dr. C. G. Somers, and the Rev. Joseph Griffiths commenced the first Sunday Schools in America, on the plan of Robert Raikes, in July, 1810, in Division street, New York.

A Sabbath School was opened in the Broadway Baptist Church, Baltimore, in 1804, two years previous to the one in Kent, supposed to be the first in the State of Maryland. This is the oldest Baptist Sunday School in the United States.

Rev. Dr. John M. Peck tells us that the first Sunday School effort in the Valley of the Mississippi was made by the missionaries under the Baptist Board of Foreign Missions, in the French village of St Louis, in March, 1818. The population of the place was then about three thousand; one of the first scholars, Rev. B. Meachaum, became a minister of the gospel. After twenty-six years services, in 1854 he fell dead in the pulpit while reading the seventeenth chapter of the gospel by St. John.

It is impossible to mention all the places where Sunday Schools were established previous to the time when our record closes. They were organized, however, in all the principal cities of the United States. In fact the societies in villages, towns, cities, counties, and states were so numerous that to give their titles would occupy much space; I shall therefore notice only the principal ones. I have already given an account of the First day or Sunday School Society formed in Philadelphia, in 1791. This Society was to America what the First Society formed in London, in 1785, was to England. Both employed paid teachers, and conducted their business in rather antiquated style until others more progressive would spring up and take the lead. The London Sunday School Union, with its four London Auxiliaries, took the front rank there in 1803.

Notwithstanding many small societies and some state unions were formed in America after the Philadelphia Society of 1791, the wants of Sabbath Schools were not fully supplied until the organization of the Philadelphia Sunday and Adult School Union, in 1817. As soon as this Society was organized, it entered vigorously upon its work; its first annual report, in 1818, shows that it had under its care forty-three schools, five hundred and fifty-six teachers, and five thousand nine hundred and seventy scholars. Their increase was gradual, but always large until 1824, when the total number of teachers and pupils amounted to nearly fifty-seven thousand, located in seventeen of the twenty-four states. Of the aggregate number, many Societies and Unions had dissolved their distinct organization and become merged into the Philadelphia Sunday and Adult School Union. Meantime the most cordial friendship existed between this and the First Day Society of 1791, that Society having paid over three hundred dollars to the Union for the support of its Schools. The tendency from the organization of the Union in 1817, had been to merge everything in the United States to a common centre, but this Union from some cause did not seem fully to satisfy the friends of Sabbath Schools. The idea of a Society still more national in its character had taken hold of their minds, and after correspondence on the subject, and a printed plan had been distributed for consideration, and the attendance of delegates from various and different Societies had been solicited, a general meeting was held December 11, 1823, in the city of Philadelphia, when the expediency of forming a National Society was determined on, and the whole subject referred to the ensuing annual meeting of the Philadelphia Sunday and Adult School Union. Accordingly, May 25, 1824, at the seventh Anniversary of the Sunday and Adult School Union, a constitution for a Society to be called the "American Sunday School Union," having been prepared, was presented to the meeting and adopted. All the property of the Sunday and Adult School Union, amounting to upwards of five thousand dollars, was then transferred by unanimous vote to the new institution. The General Assembly of the Presbyterian Church of the United States of America (that being eleven years before the division of that body into Old and New School) was in session at the time, and its members participated in the exercises.

In the last report of the Sunday and Adult School Union, they say that in the year just closed they have published two hundred and ten thousand and five hundred books, tracts, and papers, for the use of Sunday Schools. One of the first acts of the new board of managers of the American Sunday School Union was to establish a periodical called the "American Sunday School Magazine."

At the first annual meeting of the Union, May 24, 1825, it was shown that its operations amounted to near ten thousand dollars, the receipts and expenditures being about equal. A few independent Unions and Societies still prosecuted their work separately from the National Union, but they were mostly denominational.

From the number of weaker Societies which, as appears from the following paragraph, became auxiliaries to the Union, will be seen the estimation in which it was held:

"There are in connection with this Society three hundred and twenty-one auxiliaries, one thousand one hundred and fifty Schools, eleven thousand two hundred and ninety-five teachers, and eighty-two thousand six hundred and ninety-seven scholars."

"Of Sunday scholars not connected with the American Sunday School Union, there are in our country according to the best estimate we have been able to form about forty-five thousand, which added to the eighty-two thousand under your care, make the total amount one hundred and twenty-seven thousand Sunday scholars in the United States of America."

The publications of the Union for the first year in books, tracts, catechisms, almanacs, tickets, cards, and annual reports amounted to over one million copies.

Although the second annual report of the American Sunday School Union, May 23, 1826, takes a little further than our limits for this volume, (the date of the death of William Fox, April 1, 1826), yet we will give a synopsis of it. The receipts and expenditures for this year are a little more than sixteen thousand dollars. They report four hundred auxiliary Societies, with two thousand one hundred and thirty-one Schools, nineteen thousand two hundred and ninety-eight teachers, and one hundred and thirty-five thousand and seventy-four scholars. Four hundred and sixty-eight teachers and thirty-two scholars are reported as having become hopefully pious during the year. The publications of the Society are about the same as the year previous. During the year they have increased the stereotype plates from 1,000 to 3,181 pages, and have added a bindery to the establishment. The Union was organized and its two first anniversaries held in the First Presbyterian Church, Philadelphia, of which the Rev. Albert Barnes is pastor. We have brought the history of Sunday Schools in America down to the point we intended in the outset. We must give one more look at Europe.

I scarcely mentioned Scotland when noticing the European Sunday Schools in the early part of this work, for the reason that they have less need of Sabbath Schools there than in any other country perhaps in the world, the religious training of children as well as their general education being better attended to there than in any other country. Long before England was in earnest on the subject of educating the masses, even if that can be said to be the case now, Scotland had her parochial week-day Schools, answering the same purpose as our free Schools, and at the same time, had Sabbath evening Schools for giving religious instruction to those who were neglected at home and would not otherwise be provided for. When Sabbath Schools began to flourish in other places, the only perceptible influence it had upon the Scotch people was to increase the Sabbath evening Schools. In the Edinburgh Missionary Magazine for 1797, edited by the Rev. Greville Ewing, he says :—" We are happy to learn that a scheme is at present in contemplation for increasing the number of Sabbath evening Schools, for the religious instruction of children. About six months ago, many of the praying Societies of various denominations in Edinburgh and its vicinity, established a monthly meeting for prayer for the revival of religion at home, and for the success of the Gospel abroad. That actual exertion might accompany their prayers, they have formed a new Society for erecting and conducting Sabbath evening Schools in places where they appear most necessary ; and have resolved that teachers shall be provided from among themselves, who shall officiate gratis; and that members of the Society shall regularly attend, to assist the teachers in keeping the children in order."

Thirty-four of those schools were established during that year, under the auspices of that Society, and others in different parts of the country, and their good effects were apperent to all. There was one peculiarity about the Scotch Sabbath Schools ; the parents attended them in large numbers, which contributed largely to the opening of new houses of worship.

We will now turn to the Societies in England. May 9, 1826, the London Sunday School Union held its twenty-third anniversary ; it had in addition to its four London auxiliaries, a number of country Unions in England and Wales, also the Sunnday School Union for Scotland as auxiliaries. The London Union had sold in the year just closed, more than three quarters of a million copies of its publications, amounting to twenty-one thousand three hundred and seventy dollars. The number of Schools in connection with the Union and its auxiliaries was six thouand two hundred and ninety, of teachers, sixty thousand six hundred and eighty-five, of pupils, six hundred and eighty-eight thousand two hundred and eight.

The Irish Sunday School Society, founded in 1809, assisted but two schools the first year of its existence, but in 1826 there were one thousand eight hundred and four schools, thirteen thousand two hundred and fifty-five teachers, and one hundred and fifty-two thousand three hundred and ninety-one scholars under its care.

The London Hibernian Society had eleven hundred and forty-seven schools, containing ninety-four thousand two hundred and sixty-two pupils, of whom fifty thousand were children of Roman Catholics.

In connection with these societies there are over one million of children, and teachers, and every department is in the highest sate of prosperity; but where, the reader will ask, is the original Society of Sept. 7, 1785, the mother of all others?

I have before me a copy of the London Sunday School Teacher's Magazine, for May, 1830, containing the forty-fourth annual report of the old Society, and although it comes down four years further than I intended, I cannot refrain from noticing its contents. The number in attendence at this meeting, was said to be larger than at any previous meeting ; and its usefulness was increasing. It had two hundred and fifty-three schools, containing twenty-four thousand and forty-six scholars under its care. It reports the total of books issued during the year, to be, primers and alphabetical books, sixty-four thousand two hundred and forty-seven ; Testaments, seven thousand four hundred and four ; Bibles, one thousand nine hundred. Total of books from commencement of the Society ; spelling books, eight hundred and forty thousand eight hundred and fifty-five ; Testaments, one hundred and thirty-six thousand eight hundred and forty-five ; Bibles, twelve thousand one hundred and eighty-nine. The expenditures of the society for that year was more than its regular income, but it had received during the year, legacies amounting to nearly one thousand three hundred pounds. Although its scale of operations, compared with some of its daughters, was small, the old society, as appears from its report, possessed life and vigor, and seemed to relish the work as much as any of the younger organizations. The example set by Willian Fox, in the organization of this society, was imitated in almost a thousand instances before his death. But how much remains to be done. If Zion is to be enlarged, if she is to extend her borders, and circumscribe those of the great adversary, her ranks must be be filled with, and her battles fought by youthful soldiers. These must be enlisted in our Sabbath Schools, and disciplined in the Church through union of effort, and union of prayers.

The plan of this work does not admit of any extended notice of the progress of Sabbath Schools later than the year 1826. Believing that their history from that time to the present, would give ample scope to the talents of some one better qualified than the writer, he leaves the subject with the pleasing thought that in 1863, there is probably not a parish in Protestant Christendom, without its Sabbath School, and that many places where the voice of the living minister of Christ has never been heard, have been blessed by the smiling face, and cheerful voice of the Sabbath School teachers, as it were a forerunner of those who were soon to herald the glad tidings of salvation. We therefore close with the following, which appeared in the December number of the American Sunday School Magazine for 1824. It is as appropriate now, as it was then.

ADVERTISEMENT EXTRAORDINARY.

PLENTY OF WORK AND SCARCITY OF HANDS.

WANTED,

From January, 1825, to the end of the world.

A vast number of active young men and women, of "*a right spirit*" who are not afraid to work;—sober, watchful, diligent, and perserving—not *slothful* in business, but *fervent* in spirit. In character, *meek*, *patient*, and humble, studying to show themselves approved unto God,—such as need not be ashamed of their work, "apt to teach,"—in *meekness* instructing the *blind*, and ignorant, till they through repentance, shall acknowledge the *truth*. No idlers—no sluggards—none that "putting their hand to the plough will look back," but such as will find it "meat and drink to do their Master's will." Plenty of work! *Powerful* enemies to subdue—great *opposition* and *difficulties* to encounter—sin and its attendant wretchedness gaining ground daily with alarming strides—THOUSANDS OF CHILDREN IN THE SUNDAY SCHOOLS *perishing* for *lack of wisdom*, many eager to hear and learn the words of eternal life—in some places fifty or sixty collected together, and *none* to teach them!—Hark! the groans of deep distress from the wretched abodes of poverty and want.—See pale sickness stretched languishing on the humble couch of miserable straw.—See the death-struck sinner—alarmed at the approach of the king of terrors—with pallid countenance he stretches his nerveless arm, and calls for the soft hand of humanity and *Christian love* to wipe off the tear of anguish, and point to realms of endless life and bliss. From your lethargy, ye lazy Christitns, arouse ! and come to work. Let none say, "I pray the have me excused ; I cannot come." Such as thus plead, let them call to mind their divine *instructions*—" To do good and to *communicate forget not*," "for with such *sacrifices* God is *well pleased*." Such as cannot give, may lend—their time—their money—or their talents of wisdom ; and they shall be repaid, receiving four-fold, "good measure meted unto them, pressed down, and running over." If not a talent of gold, give a talent of silver ; or, as the poor widow, bestow thy two mites, into the treasury of the Lord. Something *must* be done—the foundation is laid on "the precious corner-stone," and the building must be raised—for the *master calls*, crying, "Do thy work *quickly*, for the NIGHT COMETH !" Come ye who would make an offering to the Lord and sacrifice present comforts for future blessings and eternal good—"*enduring* the *Cross* and despising the shame, for the joy set before you."—Leave all and follow *us*—*now* is the *accepted* time. Our Prince goeth to a far country, and says, "occupy till I come." Hark ! He speaks to thee from heaven—"has no man hired thee?" Enter into my vineyard—ye that "are ready to halt"—"of little faith"—"doubting"—it is the ELEVENTH HOUR—"forget the things which are behind" and press forward; for it is "*a high calling*," and the reward is *sure;* for it is of *grace* and mercy bestowed—"He will give thee thy wages"—"An inheritance"—"a kingdom"—"a crown!" Peace and joy "in this present evil life," "and in the world to come LIFE EVERLASTING." And this commendation before his Father's face and the angels—"Well done, good and *faithful servant*, enter thou into the joy of thy Lord."

Such are the terms:—for further particulars inquire within your own hearts, and knock at the door of *Conscience*, and for *engagement*, apply at "the House of Bread in Jerusalem"—or in the highways and hedges—to the shed of the widow and fatherless—to the house of poverty and *ignorance*. *No time* to be lost. We work for ETERNITY!

"FAITH—HOPE"
and
"CHARITY"

☞ N. B.—Appiication may also be made to any of the directors of the "*American Sunday School Union*," or at several thousand Sunday Schools throughout the cities, towns, and villages of the United States of America, or if preference is given to foreign parts, any of the numerous missionary stations throughout the world—and in most parts of England, Wales, Ireland, France, Holland, and in the ancient city of Jerusalem!

Dec. 1824. F. H. & C.

THE END.

PETER PARLEY'S OWN STORY.

From the Personal Narrative of the late SAMUEL G. GOODRICH (Peter Parley).

1 vol. 16mo, illustrated, price $1.

CHILDREN'S SAYINGS;

OR, EARLY LIFE AT HOME.

By CAROLINE HADLEY. With Illustrations, by WALTER CRANE.

1 vol. square 16mo, price 75 cents.

STORIES OF OLD.

OLD TESTAMENT SERIES.

By CAROLINE HADLEY.

1 vol. 12mo, Illustrated, price $1.

STORIES OF OLD.

NEW TESTAMENT SERIES.

By CAROLINE HADLEY.

1 vol. 12mo, Illustrated, price $1.

ROSE MORTON'S JOURNAL.

A series of volumes containing Rose Morton's Journal for the several months of the year.

Each volume Illustrated, 18mo, 45 cents.

There are now ready,

ROSE MORTON'S JOURNAL FOR JANUARY.
ROSE MORTON'S JOURNAL FOR FEBRUARY.
ROSE MORTON'S JOURNAL FOR MARCH.
ROSE MORTON'S JOURNAL FOR APRIL.
ROSE MORTON'S JOURNAL FOR MAY.

WALTER'S TOUR IN THE EAST.

A Series of interesting Travels through Egypt, Palestine, Turkey, and Syria. By Rev. D. C. EDDY, D.D.

Each volume beautifully Illustrated from Designs brought from those countries.

Each volume, 16mo, price 65 cents.

There are now ready,

WALTER IN EGYPT,
WALTER IN JERUSALEM,
WALTER IN SAMARIA. (Nearly ready.)

From the New York Commercial Advertiser.

"Dr. Eddy is known as the author of 'The Percy Family,' and is a most pleasing and instructive writer for the young. The present volume is one of a series of six, describing a visit of a company of young tourists to the most interesting and sacred spots on the earth. The incidents recited and the facts presented are just such as will captivate while they instruct intelligent youth, and give even adult minds some correct ideas of Eastern countries and habits. In the present volume, Walter travels through Egypt, and his story is told in some two hundred and twenty pages; so compactly told, indeed, that not a line could have been omitted without injury. It is just the book for an intelligent child.

From the Pittsburgh Gazette.

"There are four very appropriate illustrations, representing the scenery and incidents of travel in Egypt. The volume, moreover, is well written, handsomely printed at the Riverside press, neatly bound in cloth, and therefore may be commended as a suitable holiday present,—a book that will both instruct and interest youthful readers."

From the Buffalo Express.

"This beautiful little volume is the first of a series of six, describing the visit of a company of young tourists to the most interesting and sacred spots on the earth. In the one under consideration, a number of incidents are recited, and facts presented, which will be found not only exceedingly interesting and instructive to boys and girls, but will give even adult minds some idea of the romantic East. It is elegantly bound, and illustrated with a number of finely executed wood-cuts We recommend it to the attention of parents as a most suitable and beautiful holiday present.

ABBOTT'S AMERICAN HISTORY.

A Series of American Histories for Youth, by JACOB ABBOTT.

To be completed in Twelve Volumes, 18mo, price 75 cents each. Each volume complete in itself.

Each volume will be illustrated with numerous Maps and Engravings, from original designs, by F. O. C. Darley, J. R. Chapin, G. Perkins, Charles Parsons, H. W. Herrick, E. F. Beaulieu, H. L. Stephens, and others.

This Series, by the well-known author of the "ROLLO BOOKS," "ROLLO'S TOUR IN EUROPE," "HARPER'S SERIES OF EUROPEAN HISTORIES," "THE FLORENCE STORIES," &c., will consist of the following volumes:

1. ABORIGINAL AMERICA. (Now ready.)
2. DISCOVERY OF AMERICA. (Now ready.)
3. SOUTHERN COLONIES. (Now ready.)
4. THE NORTHERN COLONIES. (Ready in August.)
5. WARS OF THE COLONIES. (Now ready.)
6. REVOLT OF THE COLONIES.
7. BOSTON IN SEVENTY-FIVE.
8. NEW YORK IN SEVENTY-SIX.
9. THE CAROLINAS IN SEVENTY-NINE.
10. CAMPAIGN IN THE JERSEYS.
11. BURGOYNE AND CORNWALLIS.
12. THE FEDERAL CONSTITUTION.

NOTICES OF THE INITIAL VOLUME.

From the Boston Traveller.

"The most excellent publication of the kind ever undertaken."

From the Boston Advertiser.

"The illustrations are well designed and executed."

From the Boston Post.

"One of the most useful of the many good and popular books of which Mr. Abbott is the author."

From the Philadelphia North American.

"It is indeed a very vivid and comprehensive presentation of the physical aspect and aboriginal life visible on this continent, before the discovery by white men."

From the Troy Whig.

"Mr. Abbott's stories have for years been the delight of thousands."

THE ROLLO STORY BOOKS.

By Jacob Abbott.

Trouble on the Mountain,
Causey Building,
Apple Gathering,
The Two Wheelbarrows,
Blueberrying,
The Freshet,
Georgie,
Rollo in the Woods,
Rollo's Garden,
The Steeple Trap,
Labor Lost,
Lucy's Visit.

12 vols. 18mo. Cloth. Illustrated. Price, per set, $3.

THE FLORENCE STORIES.

By Jacob Abbott.

Vol. 1.—Florence and John. 18mo. Cloth. Illustrated.
Vol. 2.—Grimkie. 18mo. Cloth. Illustrated.
Vol. 3.—The Orkney Islands, 18mo. Cloth. Illustrated.
Vol. 4.—The Enghlish Channel. 18mo. Cloth Illustrated.
Vol. 5.—The Isle of wight, 18mo. Cloth. Illustrated.

Price of each volume 70 cents.

From the Boston Journal.

"Mr. Abbott is always an entertaining writer for the young, and this story seems to us to contain more that is really suggestive and instructive than other of his recent productions. Florence and John are children who pursue their studies at home, under the care of their mother, and in the progress of the tale many useful hints are given in regard to home instruction. The main educational idea which runs through all Mr. Abbott's works, that of developing the capacities of children so as to make them self-reliant, is conspicuous in this."

From the New York Observer.

"Mr. Abbott is known to be a pure, successful and useful writer for the young and old. He is also the most popular author of juvenile books now living."

From the Boston Traveller.

"No writer of children's books, not even the renowned Peter Parley, has ever been so successful as Abbott."

www.ingramcontent.com/pod-product-compliance
Lightning Source LLC
LaVergne TN
LVHW010217110826
845151LV00004B/1117

* 9 7 8 1 4 2 5 5 2 7 8 1 5 *